Crazy

ABOUT

Cupcakes

Crazy ABOUT Cupcakes

Krystina Castella

STERLING PUBLISHING CO., INC. New York

Library of Congress Cataloging-in-Publication Data
Castella, Krystina.
Crazy about cupcakes / Krystina Castella.
p. cm.
Includes index.
ISBN-13: 978-1-4027-1994-3
ISBN-10: 1-4027-1994-9
1. Cake. I. Title.
TX771.C34 2006
641.8'653--dc22   2005032784

10   9

Book design by Helene Berinsky

Published by Sterling Publishing Co., Inc.
387 Park Avenue South, New York, NY 10016

© 2006 by Krystina Castella

Distributed in Canada by Sterling Publishing
c/o Canadian Manda Group, 165 Dufferin Street
Toronto, Ontario, Canada M6K 3H6

Distributed in the United Kingdom by GMC Distribution Services
Castle Place, 166 High Street, Lewes, East Sussex, England BN7 1XU

Distributed in Australia by Capricorn Link (Australia) Pty. Ltd.
P.O. Box 704, Windsor, NSW 2756, Australia

Printed in China
All rights reserved

Sterling ISBN-13: 978-1-4027-1994-3
ISBN-10: 1-4027-1994-9

For information about custom editions, special sales, premium and
corporate purchases, please contact Sterling Special Sales
Department at 800-805-5489 or specialsales@sterlingpub.com.

For my grandmother Madeline Lucarelli,
who taught baking as the secret to happiness.

A special thank-you to my husband, Brian,
with whom I have shared many enjoyable creative moments in the kitchen.

Acknowledgments

Thank you to my editors, Danielle Truscott, Abby Rabinowitz, and Caitlin Earley, for their great enthusiasm and support in the creation of this book. Lara Comstock for tightening the manuscript. And to photographer Ed Rudolph and his crew, Eric Staudenmaier, Amy Paliwoda, Maggie Hill-Ward, Marcella Capasso, Julie McKevitt, for their help in creating the fabulous cupcakes and images. Thanks to my family for their support. And thank you to my friends and students for eating the thousands of cupcakes, good and bad, to help edit the best for this book.

Cupcake Definition

A small, individual-sized fluffy cake that is baked in a cupcake or muffin pan. The cupcake mold can be lined with a crimped paper or foil cup, or greased and then the cupcake removed from the mold. It is then frosted and, if desired, decorated. Before eating, the paper or foil is simply peeled off. A cupcake can be served on a plate and eaten with a fork, but most of the time the best way to savor a cupcake is to just break it apart and pop it in your mouth.

● ● ●

Cupcake History

In preparing this book I have asked folklorists, food writers, and food history professors and have searched many libraries to find out where cupcakes come from. What did I find? That there is not much written about the cultural history of cupcakes. This is what I know.

The term "cupcake" is first mentioned in E. Leslie's *Receipts* of 1828. Breaking with the tradition at this time of weighing ingredients, the ingredients began to be measured in cups. According to *Baking in America* by Greg Patent, this was revolutionary because of the tremendous time it saved in the kitchen. *The Oxford Encyclopedia of Food and Drink in America* explains that the cup name had a double meaning because of the practice of baking in small containers, including teacups.

Cups were convenient because hearth ovens took a long time to bake large cakes. Gem pans, early muffin tins, were common in households around the turn of the twentieth century and cupcakes were then baked in these.

Throughout the 1900s, cupcakes became popular kids' treats partly because of their ease in baking. In the early 1900s, Hostess introduced the snack cupcake, but it didn't become the Hostess Cupcake we know today until the 1950s.

Many people associate cupcakes with the popularity of homemaking of the 1950s and 1960s, but this is a myth. Cupcakes were no more popular during that time period than they are today. More likely is that adults associate cupcakes with memories from their childhood. What is different today is that cupcakes have gone crazy! Traditionally, they were made for children in basic flavors. Today the cupcake has gone gourmet and is playful, hip, and glamorous. Over the past few years cupcake bakeries have opened around the country, with people waiting late at night in lines out the door. This craze is here to stay.

contents

Cupcakes make people smile.

It all started when I was invited to a Tiki-themed potluck and was assigned the job of "baking something." I have been known as the baker among my friends for as long as I can remember. . . .

As a child my Sundays were spent in the Brooklyn kitchen of my Italian grandmother, Grandma Lucarelli. I was taught recipes that tasted amazing and techniques that made everything look great. The love of her life was baking. She baked for the nuns at the convent down the street and delivered cakes to neighbors and friends just because there was no way she could eat everything that she baked and she loved sharing her creations. I learned from her that if I perfected baking, I could make people happy, too.

So I whipped up fabulous creations after school with my Girl Scout troop and with members of my swim team for fund-raisers. For my Sweet 16 party I made a huge cake for more than 150 people. I baked for the kids I babysat and for customers on my paper route on special occasions. In college I threw dessert parties for my friends in my tiny apartment so we could take breaks from all-night work sessions in the studio. When I met my man many years later, three thousand miles and a zillion cultures away, it wasn't surprising that he nicknamed me "Cakie."

All of this prepared me well for the day I caught the cupcake bug. That summer evening in Los Angeles preparing for my friend's Tiki party at a condo a few steps from the beach . . . I decided to make cupcakes.

Why did I choose cupcakes?

Cupcakes are friendly. Each cupcake in a batch can be different. Each has a personality. With cupcakes I could set a mood and look for the occasion.

Cupcakes are stylish. Cupcakes are a lifestyle. Kinda hip, kinda cool—and extremely fun. I can play with recipes and toppings, experiment with taste, color, form, pattern, and texture.

Cupcakes are nostalgic. They trigger memories for adults and make memories for kids. They get people talking. Everyone has a story about a cupcake. They are all surprising. Ask someone and you'll see what I mean.

Finally, cupcakes are portable. They are easy to share since they are individual cakes. And they're not as messy because you just pop them in your mouth.

The Tiki Head Cupcakes (see page 133) were a huge success. Definitely worth the effort. So when my street had a block party, I again baked cupcakes. When I was invited to an art opening, cupcakes. A friend's thirty-ninth birthday, a Halloween party, an Academy Awards party, cupcakes, cupcakes, cupcakes.

I started making them all the time. Experimenting with recipes and decorations just for fun. I shared them at the college where I teach. People would ask, "Are these someone's project?" "What's the concept?" "Can we eat them?" I got great critiques—which ones tasted good, which ones looked good, and which ones needed improvement. "Not minimalist, too much color and frosting," or "These flavors are not part of the same vernacular," or simply "Awesome."

I realized I had gone cupcake crazy and wanted to share this passion with other cupcake lovers. I decided to put all of my cupcake research, experimentation, and experience into *Crazy About Cupcakes.* An eight-year-old from my goddaughter's class offered to promote the book and help with the marketing as long as she could get paid in cupcakes. This seemed like a good endorsement.

ABOUT THIS COOKBOOK

Let's talk a little about *Crazy About Cupcakes*. The cupcakes in this book are a starting point, a visual scrapbook of imagery, recipes, and techniques. I have chosen recipes with themes as inspiration, to be used as a reference guide, as a springboard for creativity. I encourage you to explore your own cupcake recipes and various topping and filling combinations.

There are more than 300 awesome cupcake ideas contained within five chapters. Those chapters include recipes for holiday cupcakes, parties, and events and occasions, because—like many people—I bake cupcakes most often for these events. I am always creating new ideas for decorating and taste combinations that epitomize the celebration.

Sometimes I bake just because homemade cupcakes are good food, and they can be nice to eat every day, at any hour. This is the inspiration behind Chapter 4, Everyday Cupcakes. It explores cupcakes that are simple, healthy, or quick to make, so when the mood for something chocolaty, spicy, crunchy, fruity, or creamy strikes, you'll have recipes at hand so you can just whip up a batch.

I have given kids a chapter all their own. In Chapter 8, Kids' Cupcakes, children learn playful, simple ways to bake and decorate, and the recipes are based on kids' favorite flavors. These cupcakes are also good for young-at-heart adults.

For decorators wanting to expand their skills, I have included a Baking and Decorating Techniques chapter (Chapter 2). Make your cupcakes as simple or complex as you like. Follow the book exactly or experiment. All of the recipes taste great on their own or with a simple dab of frosting. To start you on your way, I have included charts that suggest different flavor combinations. For the creative innovator, I have included design elements such as templates and ingredients lists to inspire you to create cupcakes that are uniquely your own.

In writing this book I've suggested many ways you might integrate cupcakes into the various roles you play and events you plan in your life. I hope you have as much fun making these cupcakes as I did coming up with them. Good eating!

Krystina Castella
crazyaboutcupcakes.com
Los Angeles, California

chapter 1

Cupcake Basics

CUPCAKES IN THE KNOW

Cupcake Pan Sizes

Cupcake baking pans are available in three sizes: small (mini—about 2 inches), medium (regular—about 2¾ inches), and large—about 3½ inches. This variety allows you to experiment with different decorating ideas. Recipes can be baked in any size pan, but the baking time will need to be adjusted for mini and large pans. Mini cupcakes usually take 5–7 minutes less than medium-sized cupcakes, and large cupcakes usually take 5–10 minutes more than their medium-sized counterparts.

Mixers

Despite all the baking I do, I still don't own a stand mixer. Being a product designer, I appreciate how cool they look and that they work great, so if you have one, use it. I, however, use a handheld mixer. A wooden spoon also does the trick and is a pretty good workout, too.

Filling the Cupcake Liners and Pans

The cupcakes in this book can be baked in paper liners or in greased cupcake pans. Some recipes suggest one or the other, depending on the presentation. I prefer paper liners most of the time because the cupcakes are a cinch to get out of the pan, easier to handle, and stay fresh longer. Paper liners are available in a wide range of sizes, colors, and patterns, and they also can be used to expand your design repertoire.

If you would like the sides of your cupcakes to be smooth—either because you are using cupcakes as "toppers" to be completely frosted, or plan on serving the cupcakes on a plate—bake the cupcakes directly in the pan. Grease the cups with butter, margarine, shortening, cooking oil spray, or baking oil spray (a combination of oil and flour), then lightly flour the cups. You might need to release the cupcakes from the pan by carefully running a knife around the perimeters.

The amount of batter you put in the cup determines the shape of the cupcake. Cups that are two-thirds full bake into the traditional cupcake shape. If you fill the cup half full, it will rise either to the edge or slightly below it, and you will have a small, straight-top cupcake. If the cup is three-quarters full, the cupcakes will rise above the edge of the liner and expand outward. Think about which shapes and sizes work best for your designs and fill the cups accordingly.

If you intend to add Mix-Ins (see Chapter 2), such as nuts, chocolate, or fruit, after the batter is poured in the pan, fill the individual cups one-half to two-thirds full.

The recipes in this book will yield 18–24 medium cupcakes per batch. The total number of cupcakes depends on how much batter you use to fill the cups.

Some projects call for two or three cupcake recipes. If you want a lot of cupcakes, make the full amount of each recipe. If you would like fewer cupcakes when making several recipes, scale down the recipes accordingly.

STORING CUPCAKES

Store your cupcakes in an airtight plastic container in the refrigerator. They will stay fresh for several days. The only cupcakes that you will need to eat within a day of preparing are ones that use uncooked eggs in the frosting.

Cupcakes keep well in the freezer. When you have some free time, bake a batch of cupcakes and whip up some frosting. Do not frost the cupcakes. Divide the cupcakes and frosting into separate airtight containers. When you want a treat, defrost the cupcakes and frosting, ice and decorate, and serve.

TRANSPORTING CUPCAKES

When transporting cupcakes to another location for an event or gift giving, use plastic packaging designed especially for cupcakes. These containers are available through cake and restaurant supply stores and online suppliers. Sometimes I purchase the containers from the baker in my local supermarket or my neighborhood bakery. You might want to do the same. Fellow bakers are usually willing to help out.

Another good way to transport cupcakes is to place them back into a clean cupcake pan once they are frosted and decorated. Lightly cover the decorated cupcakes with aluminum foil, taking care not to spoil the tops. The pan, unlike a flat tray, prevents them from moving around in the car. When I arrive at my destination I remove the cupcakes from the pan and present them on a tray or platter.

To ensure a flawless presentation, some people choose to frost and decorate the cupcakes when they reach their destination. Pack the cupcakes, frostings, and toppings in separate plastic containers.

To sidestep the quandary of transporting finished products and add a layer of fun, incorporate the cupcake decorating into the party entertainment. Arrange a cupcake bar with a selection of frostings and toppings for guests to customize their own desserts, based own their taste preferences and design inspirations.

INGREDIENTS

Dairy

Many of the recipes in this book suggest butter as a main ingredient because I have found that using butter as the fat produces the richest cupcakes. You are welcome to substitute margarine. If you use low-fat butter or margarine, make sure it contains at least 5 grams of fat per serving.

Soften butter by removing it from the refrigerator and setting it on a counter for about 30 minutes. Softening time will vary depending on the temperature of the room—the warmer the room, the sooner the butter will soften. Softened butter will cream more easily and will more readily combine with the other ingredients.

Cream cheese, too, works best when it is softened. Cream cheese makes cupcakes creamy, sour cream makes them sour, and yogurt makes them tangy. All of these dairy ingredients can be replaced with low-fat versions.

MILK AND CREAM

When I refer to milk I mean whole milk, although you can experiment with substituting low-fat, skim, or buttermilk in these recipes. Substitutions, however, will slightly change the flavor and texture of the recipe, but the cupcakes will still turn out well. Heavy or whipping cream should be used when cream is required. Milk and cream also work best at room temperature.

EGGS

To whip full egg whites, make sure they are at room temperature and not contaminated by any yolk. Use a clean, dry bowl and beaters, and be careful not to overbeat. Stop beating before the eggs form separate puffs. Beaten egg whites will deflate quickly, so use them immediately.

Baking Powder and Baking Soda

Baking powder and baking soda are the magic in the recipe. These ingredients make your cupcakes rise. Baking powder is a combination of baking soda plus a few other things that, when added to a batter and heated, produce a gas for leavening. If you have only baking soda, you can make your own baking powder. To make 1 teaspoon of baking powder, combine ½ teaspoon cream of tartar, ¼ teaspoon baking soda, and ¼ teaspoon cornstarch.

Sugar

Many cupcake recipes call for white granulated sugar, brown sugar, or both. Always measure sugar by dipping the measuring cup into the sugar and leveling the cup by scraping the overflow back into the container. When a recipe calls for brown sugar, you can use light or dark varieties. When measuring brown sugar, always pack it firmly into a measuring cup and level the top. Brown sugars sometimes harden so you might need to regrind the sugar in a food processor or heat it in the oven for a few minutes at 350°F to soften it.

Frosting and icing recipes call for confectioners' sugar, which is the same as powdered sugar. Making frosting with confectioners' sugar is not an exact science. You might need to adjust the recipes by adding a little more sugar or liquid to reach your desired spreading consistency.

Vanilla, Extracts, and Liqueurs

Vanilla extract comes in natural and artificial varieties. The natural form tastes much better than the artificial one, but it is more expensive and sometimes less available, so in a pinch you can substitute artificial vanilla.

Almond, peppermint, anise, and other extracts are very good flavorings for cupcakes. They do not store for very long, though, so buying the smallest bottle is wise unless you're planning to make cupcakes all of the time, like me.

Since many of these cupcakes are for parties, holidays, and other special occasions, I have included recipes using liqueurs, though these recipes can be used anytime. If you do not like the taste of the liqueur, you can leave it out and prepare the rest of the recipe as directed. Liqueurs keep for a long time, but if you will not be using them often, you can buy mini bottles.

Spices

Dried spices like cinnamon, ginger, nutmeg, and cloves keep best when purchased in small containers. Different brands have very different qualities and prices, so choose the best that you can afford. Store them in a cool dark place.

Coconut

Whole coconuts are available fresh and can be shredded on a grater or in a food processor. Dried or desiccated coconut is available shredded and flaked. Shredded coconut is more common than flaked, but either can be used in these recipes. Dried coconut comes sweetened or unsweetened. Sweetened is more common. If you're using sweetened coconut, you might want to scale down the sugar used in the recipe, depending on your sweet tooth. Toasted coconut radically changes the flavor of cupcakes and frostings. Frozen coconut, shredded or flaked, can also be used in any of these recipes. Coconut basically tastes great no matter what form you use.

Fruits

FRESH FRUITS

It is best to use fresh fruits in these recipes because frozen fruits tend to have more water. Frozen fruits will work fine if you need to substitute, but you might need to reduce the amount of liquid slightly. Berries such as cranberries and blueberries are readily available and cost effective for only a month or two every year, so you might consider buying them when they are in season and freezing them for baking later.

DRIED FRUITS

If fresh fruits are not available, you can substitute dried fruits. Dried pineapple and apricots are sweet and add an interesting texture to cupcakes. Raisins are the most popular dried fruit. Try using brown or golden raisins for different tastes.

Jams and Jellies

Choose high-quality brands because the cheaper ones contain a large percentage of corn syrup, which is used for thickening and sweetening. Heat jam with a little water to make a great glaze, filling, or frosting for your cupcakes.

Nuts

Nuts work really well for flavoring and decorating cupcakes. However, nuts are a very common allergen, so consider this when deciding whether or not to include them in your recipe. You might want to divide the batch and make some cupcakes with and some without nuts. Just make sure not to cross-contaminate the nut-free batch with a bowl or spoon used to make a nut batch. Nuts are perishable, so store them in airtight bags in the freezer. Defrost nuts before chopping. You also can toast them to a light brown, then chop them with a knife or pulverize them in a food processor.

Maple Syrup and Honey

Imitation pancake syrup is not as good as pure maple syrup and is much sweeter. You can use it if you like your cupcakes extra sweet. I prefer grade A or B amber pure maple syrup.

Honey is available in different flavors, depending on which flowers the bees pollinated. If you would like your cupcakes to have a touch of orange flavor, use orange blossom honey. Or use sage honey or clover honey. Don't worry about buying too much; as long as you store it in a cool, dry dark place, it will keep forever. You can pass it down for generations. Archaeologists have even found edible honey in Egyptian tombs.

Chocolate and Cocoa Powder

What can I say about chocolate? I cannot describe how amazing it is. Dark, milk, white, semisweet, German, unsweetened, bittersweet—there are so many kinds. It also comes in numerous shapes—bars, chunks, and chips, to name the most common. You may substitute your favorite chocolate in a recipe to suit your taste. For example, chocolate chunks can be substituted for chocolate chips, white chocolate can be substituted for semisweet. Dutch-processed or regular cocoa powder work well for these recipes. In a bind I have also substituted high-quality hot cocoa or Mexican chocolate, which is presweetened, but if you choose to do this, remember to scale down the amount of sugar in the recipe.

SUBSTITUTIONS

Substituting Ingredients

I really don't like it when cookbooks demand that you use specific ingredients, especially ones that don't fit my diet or are hard to find. I wind up making only the recipes that include ingredients I like or have in the house, and I never try the others. That is why in creating these recipes I tried many different substitutions, such as margarine for butter, low-fat milk for whole milk, and frozen fruit for fresh fruit. Although substitutions may alter the taste and texture of the cupcakes, they will still be tasty and will fit your lifestyle better. Substitutions are suggested in the Ingredients section of each recipe.

Substituting Recipes

Most recipes in this book are interchangeable. You may also choose to substitute your own favorite recipes for the cupcake or frosting recipe that I have chosen for a particular design. For example, I have created a Champagne Cupcakes recipe for New Year's Eve, a pumpkin recipe for Halloween, and a lemon recipe for Easter. These recipes suit the occasions well. If you like the design but want to choose your favorite recipes, go right ahead and then follow the decorating instructions.

Substituting Prepared Ingredients

If you are short on time, use cake mixes, store-bought cupcakes, or prepared frosting. This will allow more time for decorating

Store-bought equivalents of some toppings can be substituted for the homemade kind. Good examples are alphabet cookies, marzipan, gingerbread men, rice cereal–and–marshmallow treats, caramel topping, marshmallow cream, whipped cream, or hot fudge.

chapter 2

Baking and Decorating Techniques

BAKING TECHNIQUES

Marbleized Cupcakes

Here are two ways to marbleize cupcakes for flavor:

1. Once the batters (for instance, a vanilla and a chocolate) are prepared they can be loosely swirled together with a spatula in a mixing bowl. The batter can then be carefully poured into the cupcake liners. Bake as directed. If the cupcakes have different baking times, find the average time of the two recipes.
2. Pour one batter into cupcake liner, filling it one-third full, then pour the other batter on top. With a knife, loosely swirl the flavors together. Bake as directed.

Layered Cupcakes

Here are two ways to layer cupcakes for flavor:

1. Pour one batter into cupcake liners until one-third full. Then pour the other batter on top until two-thirds full. Bake as directed.
2. Fill cupcake liners with one batter until three-quarters full. These

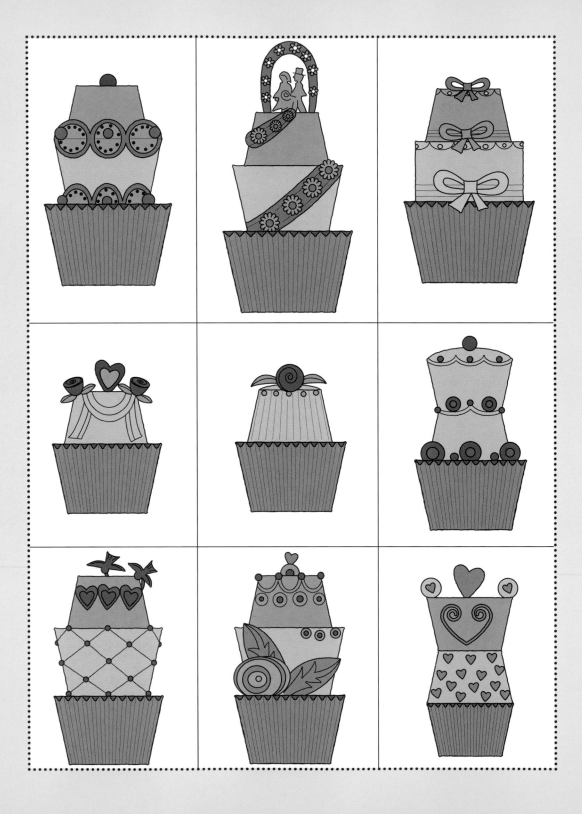

will be your bottom layers. Fill a greased cupcake pan with the second batter. These will be your top layers. Make the same amount of top layers as bottom layers. Bake as directed. When cool, frost the bottom layer. Turn the top-layer cupcakes upside down and glue with frosting to bottom layers. Frost the top layer.

Tiered Cupcakes

These are my favorite cupcakes to make. A tiered cupcake is made of two or more layers of cake, either using multiple cupcakes of the same size or various graduated sizes. Each tier is attached with frosting or jam. Using different-sized cupcake pans makes it easy to experiment with building unique cupcake forms.

Tiered cupcakes are a great way to mix flavors; just choose a different cupcake recipe for each tier. Remember you will need two or three cupcakes for every completed tiered cupcake, so keep this in mind when preparing the batter. If using one recipe, you might want to double the batch. You can also divide the recipes as needed.

Bake the bottom layers in paper liners. The upper tiers can be baked either in a greased-and-floured cupcake pan or in paper liners that are removed when the cupcakes are cool. If the design suggests that upper layers be square, bake them in a square or rectangular cake pan, then cut the cake into graduated size squares. When pouring batter into the pans or cutting squares, keep track of how many of each layer you are making and be sure you have enough of each size for bottom, middle, and top layers.

When frosting tiered cupcakes, frost the lower tier first, then the sides of the second tier, and then the top. Frost the sides of the third tier, then the top, and so on. Using different-colored frostings for the tiers or sides and tops is a playful way to ice tiered cupcakes.

You can decorate tiered cupcakes with store-bought toppings and use the piping patterns on the opposite page specifically designed for tiered cupcakes.

Mix-In Cupcakes

Adding mix-in ingredients such as nuts, chocolates, fruits, and candies to the batter is a simple way to create taste variations within one batch of cupcakes. For suggestions of mix-in ingredients check the list on page 247. Here are simple mix-in cupcakes and frosting methods.

MIX-IN CUPCAKES METHOD
1. Prepare the cupcake batter.
2. Fill the cupcake liners one-half to two-thirds full with batter.
3. Add different mix-ins to cupcakes by pushing ingredients slightly into batter with a teaspoon. Bake the cupcakes.

MIX-IN FROSTING METHOD
1. Prepare the frosting.
2. Divide the frosting into several small bowls.
3. Add different mix-ins into each bowl. Mix the frostings.
4. Frost the cupcakes when cool.

Ice Cream Cupcakes

ORIGINAL ICE CREAM CUPCAKES METHOD
1. Use a small scoop or melon baller to place a small scoop of ice cream on tops of medium-sized cupcakes.
2. Sprinkle toppings over the ice cream. Serve immediately.

LARGE ICE CREAM CUPCAKES METHOD
1. Remove two teaspoons of cake from the center of cupcakes with a grapefruit spoon.
2. Scoop ice cream into the hole, pour in sauce, and sprinkle toppings over the ice cream. Serve immediately.

DECORATING TECHNIQUES

Frosting Techniques and Textures

Most cupcakes will need to be cooled for about 30 minutes before you frost them, otherwise the frosting will melt.

When it comes to frosting, icing, and ganache, consistency is everything. Different types of frosting have different textures. Frosting is thicker than icing; ganache is a glaze, usually made of chocolate. If your frosting or icing is too soft, it will slide off the cupcakes; if it is too firm, it will stick to and tear the cupcakes.

For frosting, you want a smooth, spreadable consistency, so that you can make thick swirling textures. When using a pastry bag with a large tip, always use frosting, not icing. If frosting is too soft, chill it briefly. If frosting is too hard, warm it to room temperature or beat it.

Icing is thin and sometimes hardens. Icing can be applied with a knife if you use a circular motion and work your way from the center toward the cupcake perimeter. If your frosting doesn't turn out perfectly, cover it with chopped nuts, coconut, nonpareils, colored sugar, or other toppings of your choice.

BULL'S-EYE PATTERNS

Using a butter knife or frosting spatula, frost the center circle first and then the other loops in alternating colors.

TWO-TONED PATTERNS

Place a dollop of colored frosting on one side of the cupcake, then a dollop of the other color on the other side. Using a clean knife for each color, spread the frostings across each half of the cupcake. Use the tip of one knife to create a sharp, clean line where the colors meet.

SWIRLED PATTERNS

Place two dollops of frosting—one dollop each of two different colors—on the cupcakes and gently mix them together with a knife.

WAVES

First apply blue frosting with a knife. Place the bottom of the knife on the frosting and lift up to create points. Make whitecaps by putting white frosting on a toothpick and applying it to the points.

CLOUDS

Apply blue frosting for the sky and swirl white frosting on top.

"SAND" AND "DIRT"

Apply frosting in uneven clumps. Dust with granola, nuts, ground graham crackers, or finely crushed chocolate cookies.

Food Coloring

Many types of food coloring can be used for frosting, icing, and cupcake batter. Liquid food coloring is the most popular and you can find it in most grocery stores. Remember, white frosting is usually your base, so the color on the bottle will be darker than your final frosting. To achieve light colors, add only a few drops; to make deep colors, add several drops. Adding food coloring will thin the icing, so you may need to add more confectioners' sugar to reach desired spreading or piping consistency.

Gel and paste food coloring are highly concentrated; you need only a little bit to achieve dark or bright colors. They are available online or at restaurant or cake decorating supply stores. If you want to make black or dark-colored frosting, start with chocolate frosting and add coloring gels.

Powdered food coloring can be brushed on by combining powders with water or lemon extract. You can purchase powdered food coloring in metallic, iridescent, or deep colors.

Precolored icings and decorating gels are available in many supermarkets, cake decorating shops, and crafts stores. These products are packaged in tubes, are ready to use, and eliminate the need for a pastry bag.

FROSTING COLOR WHEEL AND PALETTES

This color wheel is a chart for mixing food colorings to achieve a desired result. The color palettes are suggestions of color schemes to help produce an occasion-specific "look" for your cupcakes.

Stenciling

Stenciling can be used on frosted or unfrosted cupcakes. Refer to Chapter 9, Flavor Combinations and Design Elements, for sample stencil templates. Here's how to make and use stencils:

1. Cut a circle a little larger than your cupcakes from a piece of card stock.
2. Draw a pattern onto the card stock and cut the circle out. With a utility knife, cut the pattern within the stencil. You can also fold the circle in quarters or eighths and cut out shapes as if you were creating a paper snowflake.

Color Wheel

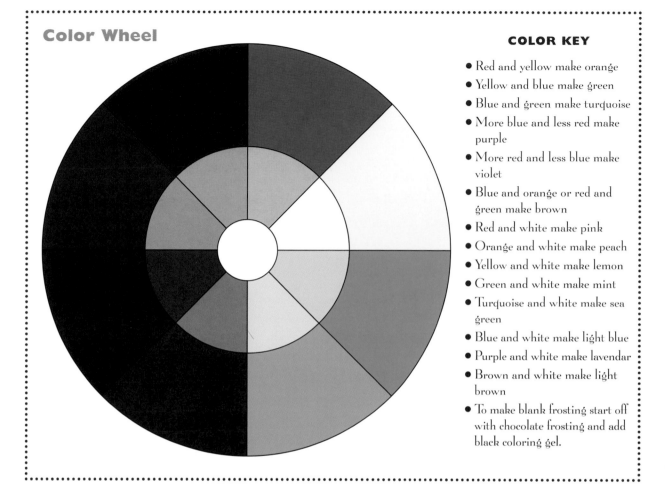

COLOR KEY

- Red and yellow make orange
- Yellow and blue make green
- Blue and green make turquoise
- More blue and less red make purple
- More red and less blue make violet
- Blue and orange or red and green make brown
- Red and white make pink
- Orange and white make peach
- Yellow and white make lemon
- Green and white make mint
- Turquoise and white make sea green
- Blue and white make light blue
- Purple and white make lavendar
- Brown and white make light brown
- To make blank frosting start off with chocolate frosting and add black coloring gel.

3. Sift powdered cocoa or powdered sugar over the stencil and onto the cupcakes.

Gold Leafing

Gold leaf is edible and makes a rich decoration on cupcakes. Just don't eat it every day. Apply it over smooth frosting with a brush or in tiny pieces by hand.

Decorating the Liners

Once your cupcakes are baked you can decorate the liners by attaching paper cutouts or ribbons with white glue or a hot glue gun. Measure the diameter of your cupcakes and make a template. Then cut the ribbons or cutouts in the desired shapes. Wrap them around the liners and glue them, taking care not to let glue come into contact with anything edible.

DECORATING TOOLS

Knives and Spatulas

Typically you will frost the cupcakes with a butter knife or cupcake-sized stainless steel frosting spatula. Reserving a separate spreading tool for each color makes frosting cupcakes go quickly.

Paintbrushes

Paintbrushes can be used to smooth out frosting or to paint on liquid or powdered food coloring. Though synthetic brushes work, soft natural brushes will last forever and are superior.

Pastry Bags

For sculpting and shaping frosting you will use a pastry bag. They can be purchased in either disposable or reusable varieties. Polyester pastry bags are recommended over cloth ones because they are easier to clean. Disposable bags do the trick but they may break easily.

It may seem intimidating to draw or write with a pastry bag, but don't worry, anyone can do it with a little practice. You can try making shapes on a plate and then scoop the frosting up to reuse once you have perfected your technique.

Remember, frosting must be the correct consistency. If it is too firm, it will be hard to push through the tip; if it is too soft, it will not hold its shape. Add a little confectioners' sugar to frosting if it is too thin. If it is too thick, add a little liquid such as milk or water.

There are hundreds of decorating tips available. You might want to purchase a basic set or, instead, maybe a few individual tips in the popular writing, round, and star shapes to get started. Small tips are great for detailed designs and royal icing. Use larger tips for buttercream icings and frosting. Here's how to use a pastry bag:

1. Choose your tip shape and place the tip into the bag. Different shaped tips will require holding the bag straight or at an angle. Secure the tip into the bag with a coupler.
2. Fill the bag one-half to two-thirds full with frosting. Fold over or twist the back portion of the pastry bag to prevent the frosting from drying and hardening or from squeezing out the back.
3. With your hands, squeeze the sides of the bag until the frosting emerges from the tip onto the cupcake. Control the flow of the frosting to create the desired shape.
4. Practice, practice, practice.

BOLD SHAPES

Frost cupcake tops with thick frosting. With a large tip make bold shapes like circles or spirals on the cupcake.

DELICATE DESIGNS

Frost cupcake tops with thin icing. Use a small writing tip to create detailed delicate designs such as lines, spirals, and circles.

STARS

Choose a star-shaped tip in the size that best suits your design. Holding the piping bag upright, gently squeeze the bag to release the frosting and form a star. Pull the bag away quickly to make a neat point on the star.

TWISTED ROPES

Choose a rope tip in the size your design requires. Hold the bag at a slight angle and pipe a continuous line with even pressure, twisting the bag as you pipe.

TRAILS

Insert a small round tip into your pastry bag. Hold the bag at a 45-degree angle against the cupcake. Apply pressure to form the icing into a dot. Then move the tip from left to right (or right to left if you're a lefty), starting and stopping at consistent intervals to create a line of dots.

SHELLS

Using a star tip, press the tip of the bag on the surface of the cupcake at your starting point. Gently squeeze the bag, lifting it up, then down, ending at the surface of the cupcake every half-inch to inch from the starting point. Pull tip away from the frosting. Start your next shell where the last one left off and continue around the cupcake.

DOTS

Using a pastry bag with a writing tip, hold the bag over the area you wish to decorate. Press out the frosting so it forms a dot. Release the pressure on the bag and detach the bag from the dot. Sometimes points will form as a result; to reduce these points, touch with a damp paintbrush to flatten them. One playful technique is to make multi-level dots: First make large dots with a large tip and then overpipe with smaller dots using a small tip.

LINES, LOOPS, ZIGZAGS, AND TRELLISES

The smaller the hole on a writing tip, the finer the line. Choose a tip to match the line size you would like to make. Rest the tip at your starting point on the cupcake. Hold the bag at an angle and pipe out a little frosting, lifting the bag slightly above the surface as you continue. Do not pull on the line; it will break. When you reach the end of the line, release the pressure on the bag. Create loops, zig-zags, and curves with your lines. You can also create a grid or trellis by overlapping lines.

OVERPIPING

To create more elaborate textures, pipe one design over another using different techniques. Use a larger tip for the first piping and a smaller one for the overpiping. Choose two different colors of icing to create detailed designs.

STITCHING

If you would like your piping to look like embroidery or stitching, use a small writing tip. Hold the tip against the cupcake. Press some frosting out of the pastry bag while moving your hand and lifting it slightly, then press the tip against the cupcake again. Repeat, moving your hand up and down from the cupcake top to create stitches.

WORDS

Words are created like doodling. For cursive writing, use a small writing tip to pipe a continuous flow of frosting to create letters just as you would if you were writing with a pencil.

FLOWERS

Place a petal tip into your piping bag. Pipe about five flat petals in a circle so they overlap each other. Pipe different colored dots in the center.

LEAVES

It is nice to add leaves to your flowers because it will make the flowers look more realistic. Hold the bag at a 45-degree angle to the cupcake. Without moving the tip, squeeze the bag and allow the frosting to fan out. Lessen your pressure as you pull the tip away to form a point on the leaf.

OTHER DESIGNS

On page 34 are different piping designs that can be achieved with the many tips available.

CHOCOLATE TECHNIQUES

Melting Chocolate

The best way to melt chocolate is in a double boiler. If you don't own one, create a double boiler by placing a bowl over a saucepan containing boiling water. Do not allow the bowl to touch the water. Also be sure that your bowl is absolutely dry inside; even a single dot of water in the bowl will seize the chocolate. When your double boiler is assembled:

1. Break the chocolate into small pieces or start off with chocolate chips. Slowly melt the chocolate, stirring occasionally.
2. When the chocolate has melted, remove it from the heat and stir.

Chocolate can also be melted in a microwave, though the timing is hard to control. Here's how to do it:

1. Place the chocolate in a clean, dry bowl and heat for thirty seconds. Check to see if the chocolate is melted. If not, heat for another thirty seconds or for smaller time increments until the chocolate is melted.
2. When chocolate has melted, remove it from the microwave and stir.

Piped Chocolate

Chocolate can be piped directly onto cupcakes, or it can be piped onto parchment paper, cooled, and then placed on cupcakes. You can pipe white, milk, or dark chocolate. To pipe directly on cupcakes:

1. Frost the cupcakes with frosting or icing.
2. Melt the chocolate and allow it to cool slightly. Decorate quickly because the chocolate will cool and set before you know it. Make sure it is the right consistency and not too runny, or it will not hold its shape.
3. Fit the piping bag with a small writing tip and fill it with chocolate.
4. Pipe your favorite design in a continuous line directly onto the cupcakes.

To pipe chocolate onto parchment paper:

1. Tape a piece of parchment paper flat to a cookie sheet. Draw your designs on the paper. Tape a piece of waxed paper over the drawing; it will be transparent.
2. Melt the chocolate and allow it to cool slightly.
3. Fit the piping bag with a small writing tip and fill with chocolate.
4. Pipe the chocolate in a continuous line onto the parchment paper over the designs. Let it set in a cool location.
5. When cool, gently lift the chocolate off the paper with a spatula and set it on the cupcakes.

To make chocolate shapes:

1. Tape a piece of parchment paper flat to a cookie sheet. Draw your designs on the paper with a black marker. Tape a piece of waxed paper over the drawings. You will see the drawings through the paper.
2. Melt white and dark chocolate separately and allow them to cool slightly.
3. Fit the piping bag with a small writing tip and fill with one chocolate. Outline your designs.
4. Fit another piping bag with a larger tip and the other chocolate and fill in the outline. Let it set in a cool location.
5. When cool, gently lift the chocolate off the parchment paper with a spatula and set it on the cupcakes.

Chocolate Cutouts

1. Tape a piece of parchment paper flat to a cookie sheet.
2. Pour the melted chocolate on the parchment paper and spread evenly with a spatula to about ¼-inch thickness. Allow the chocolate to cool just until firm. If you let the chocolate get too hard, it will break during the next step.
3. Press a cookie cutter into the chocolate or cut your desired shapes with a knife. Do not touch it or you will leave fingerprints. Carefully lift the chocolate from the paper with a spatula.
4. If you like, you can decorate the shapes with piped chocolate.

Chocolate Leaves

1. Pick small, real, nontoxic leaves that have prominent veins. Rose leaves work well. Leave the stems on. Wash and dry the leaves.
2. With a paintbrush, brush melted chocolate about ³⁄₁₆-inch thick onto the underside of each leaf. You can mix two colors of chocolate together to create a marbleized effect.
3. Place the leaves on waxed or parchment paper to cool. If the chocolate is too thin, brush on another coat and let set.
4. Starting at the stem, carefully peel the leaves from the chocolate and use the chocolate leaves to decorate the cupcakes.

Using Candy Molds

You can melt chocolate and pour it into candy molds to create desired shapes, such as letters, numbers, and flowers. Candy for melting is also available in a variety of colors at crafts and cake decorating stores.

Chocolate Curls and Shavings

LONG CURLS

1. Pour the melted chocolate on a cutting board. Spread evenly with a spatula to about ¼-inch thickness. Allow the chocolate to cool until firm but not too hard.
2. Shave the chocolate by holding a large knife at a 45-degree angle to the chocolate. Push the knife back and forth to make curls.
3. Lift the curls with the knife and set on the frosted cupcake. Let set until firm.

SHORT CURLS

Peel curls from a bar of chocolate with a vegetable peeler.

SHAVINGS

Grate a bar of chocolate with a grater. Different sides of the grater will produce different-sized shavings.

CHOCOLATE-COVERED FRUITS AND NUTS

1. Wash and dry the fruits. Make sure fruits are at room temperature or the chocolate will set too quickly and break.
2. Line a baking sheet with parchment or waxed paper. Hold fruits by the stems or nuts with a fork and dip halfway into the chocolate. Remove and allow excess chocolate to drip back into the bowl. Place on paper to set.
3. For dark and white chocolate dips, allow fruits or nuts to set after first dip, then dip the other half of the fruit or nut into the other flavored chocolate. Allow to set.

SUGAR PASTE ICINGS AND MARZIPAN

Cutouts

Shaping sugar paste icing or marzipan with cookie cutters is an easy way to make colorful cupcake toppings and decorations. Use circular cookie cutters to make perfect circle tops for your cupcakes. Flowers, stars, numbers, letters, and many other shapes are available. Cookie cutters come in a variety of sizes; small ones work best for cupcakes. Here's how to make cutouts:

1. Add the food coloring of choice and blend it into the sugar paste icing or marzipan.
2. Roll it out on a confectioners' sugar–dusted surface. Dip the sharp sides of the cutters into cornstarch, press into the rolled-out sugar paste or marzipan, and cut out the shapes. Shapes can also be cut out freehand with a knife.
3. Lay the cutout shapes on the cupcakes or securely attach layers of shapes together by using frosting as glue.

Embossing

A relief pattern, shape, or texture can be made on sugar paste icing or marzipan. Dust the cookie cutters, forks, or a patterned tool with a little cornstarch and gently press your pattern or shape into the icing; do not press all the way through.

Painting on Icing

Food coloring can be used as paint. Place a few drops in a palette and brush it on just as you would watercolors. Edible markers can be used to create interesting shading or line work. Powdered tints are also available for painting. Here's how to do it:

1. Allow the sugar paste icing or marzipan to dry on the cupcakes.
2. Draw your design on the cupcakes with an edible marker or emboss the design with cookie cutters. You can also use stencils cut out of card stock or plastic.
3. Dilute the food coloring with water. Mix the colors you would like to use in small cups or a plastic palette.

4. With a brush, paint on your designs in food coloring or powdered tints. Add highlights and shading with markers.

Coloring Marzipan

To color marzipan, divide the batch into balls, using one ball for each
color. Flatten balls and add a few drops of food coloring to the centers. Knead the marzipan until the color is evenly blended. Continue
to add food coloring until the desired color is achieved. When the
marzipan is dry and shaped, add details with food coloring and a
brush.

SHAPING ICINGS AND MARZIPAN

Braiding and Weaving

STRIPED ROPES

1. Dust a work surface with confectioners' sugar. Using your hands,
   roll out two strips of marzipan or sugar paste icing to equal
   width and length.
2. Pinch one end of the strips together. Twist the strips into a rope.
   When the rope is complete, pinch the other end together.

BRAIDS

1. Dust a work surface with confectioners' sugar. Using your hands,
   roll out three pieces of the same or different colored marzipan
   to equal width and length.
2. Pinch one end of the strips together. Braid the strips into a
   thicker rope. When the braid is complete, pinch the other end
   together.

BASKET WEAVES

1. Dust a work surface with confectioners' sugar. Using a rolling
   pin, roll out onto a flat surface the same or different colored
   marzipan or sugar paste strips until ¼-inch thick. Cut into sixteen ¼-inch-wide strips approximately the same length as the
   diameter of the cupcakes you are decorating.

2. To make a basket weave, lay out horizontally eight parallel strips with a ¼ inch of space between each strip. Cut eight more identical strips. Take the first of the eight new strips and weave it vertically (perpendicular to) in and out of the first eight strips. Repeat the process with all eight strips.

3. Trim the basket weave into a circle shape with a circular cookie cutter dusted with cornstarch.

Bows

1. Dust a work surface with confectioners' sugar. Roll out the sugar paste icing or marzipan until it is ¹⁄₁₆- to ⅛-inch thick. Cut two strips of desired length and form two loops. Pinch the loops together to attach in the center.

2. Now cut another strip long enough to wrap around the loops and cover the intersection.

3. Cut two more strips to create ribbon ends. Notch the ends by cutting triangles out of them. Pinch ends to the back of the bow.

Ribbons

1. Dust a work surface with confectioners' sugar. Roll out the sugar paste icing or marzipan till ¹⁄₁₆- to ⅛-inch thick. Cut strips of desired length and form several different-sized loops.

2. Pinch the loops together in an arch. Place on top of cupcakes.

Foods, Flowers, and Other Shapes

Marzipan can be shaped into fruits, vegetables, flowers, and even holiday characters. When shapes dry, add details with food coloring and a brush.

BANANAS

1. Roll yellow marzipan into tiny balls.

2. Roll into banana shapes, pressing to taper one end to a point, and bend them slightly.

3. Square off the thick ends by tapping them with your finger. Allow them to dry for an hour.

4. Paint them with green and brown food coloring, depending on how ripe you would like them to look.

CARROTS

1. Roll orange marzipan into tiny balls.
2. Roll the balls between your palms and make tapered carrot shapes. Make the tips blunt but not sharp.
3. Use the back of a knife to score indentations in the tops and lines down the edges.

PUMPKINS AND JACK-O'-LANTERNS

1. Divide the marzipan into one large ball, colored orange, and one small ball, colored green.
2. Roll orange marzipan into tiny balls.
3. Using the back of a knife, make five indentations from top to bottom around the sides of the orange balls to make pumpkin shapes.
4. Using your thumb, slightly indent the tops where the lines meet.
5. Roll the green marzipan into stalk shapes. Use a little water as glue and press the stalks into the tops of the pumpkins.
6 To make the pumpkins into jack-o'-lanterns, cut faces into the balls with a food-safe craft knife, or use a brush to paint faces with black food coloring.

STRAWBERRIES

1. Divide the marzipan into large balls, colored red, and small balls, colored green.
2. Taper one side of the red balls to resemble the strawberry shape.
3. Roll the strawberries over a grater or zester to texture the surface.
4. Shape the green marzipan into four-pointed stars by rolling two small balls, tapering the ends, and crossing them in the center. Using a bit of water as glue, attach them to the tops of the strawberries.

ORANGES

1. Roll orange marzipan into tiny balls.
2. Roll the balls over a grater or zester to texture the surface.
3. Press cloves into the tops of the oranges to make indented star-shaped patterns.

LEMONS

1. Roll yellow marzipan into tiny balls.
2. Taper both ends of the ball to make it resemble a lemon.
3. Roll the balls over a grater or zester to texture the surface.
4. Use a toothpick to create indentations in the tapered ends.
5. Allow the lemons to dry for an hour, then detail the ends with green food coloring.

LIMES

1. Roll green marzipan into tiny balls.
2. Roll the balls over a grater or zester to texture the surface.
3. Press cloves into the tops of the limes to make indented star-shaped patterns.
4. Allow the limes to dry for an hour, then paint the ends green with food coloring.

ROSES

1. Divide the marzipan into one large ball, colored your favorite shade of rose, and one smaller ball, colored green. Take the large rose-colored ball and divide the majority of it into tiny balls. The remainder will be small balls.
2. Form the small rose-colored balls of marzipan into cone shapes. These cones will support the petals.
3. Flatten the tiny rose-colored balls into petal shapes that are slightly thicker toward one end. Wrap one petal around the cone and press it in. With your fingers, curl the ends of the petal. To make a rosebud, do not curl the petals.
4. Overlap the first petal with a second petal, and repeat around the cone until a row is created. Repeat the rows around the whole cone.

5. Make pointed leaves out of flattened green marzipan. Make vein indentations and/or jagged edges with a knife.

SNOWMEN

1. Divide the marzipan into three balls: one large ball and two smaller balls. Leave the large ball plain and color the other balls black and orange.
2. Create snowmen figures by making two or three snowballs out of the plain marzipan for each. Stick them together with icing or a little water, pressing to secure.
3. Roll the orange marzipan into a sheet and cut scarf shapes out of it. Use a knife to create fringe on both ends. Wrap the scarfs around the snowmen's necks.
4. With the remaining orange marzipan, make carrot noses. Put a little water on the tips and press the carrots into the faces.
5. With the black marzipan, roll out dots for eyes, buttons, and top hats. Attach with a little water, pressing to secure.

TURKEY

1. Divide the marzipan into two large balls and two smaller balls. With food coloring, color one large ball light brown and the other dark brown. Leave one small ball white and color the other one orange.
2. To make the body, form a 1-inch ball out of the dark brown marzipan. To make the neck and head, roll a strip of light brown marzipan about ¾-inch long and attach a ½-inch round ball at the top. Join the neck and head to the body.
3. For the feathers, roll out white marzipan and the remaining light and dark brown marzipan with a rolling pin to a thickness of about ¼ inch. Cut the marzipan with flower cookie cutters of various sizes. Cut the flowers in half and attach them to the body.
4. To make the face, shape the remaining brown and white marzipan into a ¼-inch cone-shaped beak. Attach it to the face. Roll the orange marzipan into thin strips and lay them over the beak. Attach candy dot eyes, or make your own with the remaining marzipan.

Coconut and Nuts

TINTING COCONUT

Combine a few drops of water and a few drops of food coloring in a small plastic container. Add the coconut. Cover the container and shake well until all coconut is colored.

TOASTING COCONUT AND NUTS

There are two ways to toast coconut and nuts:

1. Place nuts or coconut on a cookie sheet and bake at 325°F for 7–10 minutes or until golden, tossing a few times while baking.
2. Place a little butter in a skillet. Add nuts or coconut and sauté for about 5–7 minutes or until golden.

FRUITS AND CITRUS GARNISHES

Frosted Fruits

Choose small fruits to decorate cupcakes. Strawberries, blueberries, raspberries, cranberries, cherries, grapes, and pineapple slices work well. So do orange, lemon, and lime wedges.

1. Whisk an egg white in a small bowl. Hold the fruit by its stem and brush the fruit with the egg white.
2. Sprinkle superfine sugar over the fruit with a spoon. Shake it to remove the excess. Place the fruit on paper towels in a warm place to dry.

Orange Slices and Maraschino Cherries

With a sharp knife, cut through a whole unpeeled orange on its meridian at ¼-inch intervals. The result is a set of whole circles in various diameters. You can either use a whole circle or cut the circles to make half slices. Pierce a maraschino cherry with a toothpick and slide the cherry to the middle of the toothpick. Fold the citrus slices over the edges of the toothpick.

Citrus Slices

Cut slices of different citrus fruits. Twist them together on a toothpick.

Mint Strawberries

Remove the green stems from the strawberry tops. Cut a hole in each top to insert a mint leaf.

Pineapple Maraschino Cherry Kabobs

Cut a pineapple chunk into ½-inch-thick triangular pieces. Slide onto a toothpick, alternating pineapple and maraschino cherries.

Cherry Kabobs

Cherries come in all different colors. Alternate them on a toothpick for garnish.

Bananas

Prepare these just before serving. Cut bananas into ⅜-inch-thick slices and dip into lemon juice to prevent oxidation (browning). Place onto a toothpick. Sprinkle banana with ground nutmeg and cinnamon.

Zests

Use firm clean oranges, lemons, or limes with unblemished skin for zests and garnishes.

SPIRALS

Peel a thin 4-inch-long strip of zest in a continuous spiral with a knife, vegetable peeler, or zester. Be careful not to cut into the white pith. Place on the cupcake in a spiral pattern.

KNOTS

Peel a thin 3- to 4-inch-long strip of zest with a knife, vegetable peeler, or zester. Gently tie the strip into a knot.

SHAPES

Carefully remove the entire peel from the citrus fruit. Using a cookie cutter, cut shapes from fruit peel. Place on tops of cupcakes.

A sweet selection. On cake stand, clockwise from top: Tiered Almond Cupcake, His and Her Family Cupcake (modified), Coffee Cupcake, Crystal Flower Cupcake, Presents Cupcake.

chapter 3

Recipes

CUPCAKE RECIPES

Almond Cupcakes

1¾ cups sour cream
½ pound (2 sticks) unsalted
    butter, at room temperature
½ cup walnut or vegetable oil
3½ cups all-purpose flour
1 teaspoon baking powder
1 teaspoon baking soda
½ teaspoon salt
2 cups granulated sugar
⅔ cup almonds, ground and
    toasted
4 large eggs, at room
    temperature
2 teaspoons almond extract
1 teaspoon vanilla extract

1. Preheat the oven to 325°F. Insert liners into a medium cupcake pan.

2. In a large bowl cream 1 cup of the sour cream, the butter, and the oil.

3. In a separate bowl sift together the flour, baking powder, baking soda, and salt. Stir in the sugar and almonds.

4. Add the dry ingredients to the creamed butter mixture, one-third at a time. Mix thoroughly after each addition.

5. In another bowl mix the eggs, the remaining ¾ cup of sour cream, and the almond and vanilla extracts.

6. Add the egg mixture to the batter in thirds, beating for 1 minute on medium speed after each addition.

7. Fill the cupcake liners three-quarters full with batter. Bake for 20–25 minutes or until a toothpick inserted in the center of cupcakes comes out clean. Cool cupcakes in the pan.

Apple Cupcakes

1½ cups Granny Smith
    apples, peeled and grated
1 tablespoon brandy or cognac
1¼ cups all-purpose flour
¾ cup granulated sugar
1 teaspoon baking soda
½ teaspoon salt
1 teaspoon ground cinnamon
⅛ teaspoon ground nutmeg
¼ teaspoon ground cloves
2 large eggs
½ cup vegetable oil
1 teaspoon vanilla extract

1. Preheat the oven to 350°F. Insert liners into a medium cupcake pan.

2. In a small bowl combine grated apple and brandy or cognac.

3. In a separate bowl combine the flour, sugar, baking soda, salt, cinnamon, nutmeg, and cloves.

4. Add the eggs, oil, vanilla, and apple mixture to the dry ingredients until fully integrated.

5. Fill the cupcake liners three-quarters full with batter. Bake for 20–25 minutes or until a toothpick inserted in the center of cupcakes comes out clean. Cool cupcakes in the pan.

Banana Cupcakes

½ pound (2 sticks) unsalted
    butter, at room temperature
1 cup granulated sugar
2 large eggs
1 cup mashed ripe bananas
1¾ cups all-purpose flour
1 teaspoon baking soda
½ teaspoon salt
5 tablespoons milk
2 teaspoons vanilla extract

1. Preheat the oven to 350°F. Insert liners into a medium cupcake pan.

2. With an electric mixer on medium speed, cream the butter and sugar together until fluffy, about 3–5 minutes. Add the eggs to the creamed mixture and beat well. Add the bananas and mix well.

3. In a separate bowl sift together the flour, baking soda, and salt.

4. Add all the dry ingredients to the creamed mixture and mix until completely integrated.

5. Add the milk and vanilla. Mix for 1 minute on medium speed.

6. Fill cupcake liners one-half to three-quarters full with batter. Bake for 20–25 minutes or until a toothpick inserted in the center of cupcakes comes out clean. Cool cupcakes in the pan.

Bittersweet Molten Chocolate Cupcakes

1/4 pound plus 2 tablespoons
   (1 1/4 sticks) unsalted butter
1/2 cup plus 2 tablespoons
   (5 ounces) bittersweet
   chocolate, chopped
3 large eggs
3 large egg yolks
1/4 cup granulated sugar
3 tablespoons all-purpose flour

1. Preheat the oven to 350°F. Insert liners into a cupcake pan.

2. In the top of a double boiler melt the butter and chocolate together. Cool for 5 minutes.

3. In a large mixing bowl beat the eggs, egg yolks, and sugar with an electric mixer at medium speed until yellow, thick, and creamy, about 5 minutes.

4. Fold the egg mixture into the melted chocolate-butter mixture until fully integrated. Fold in the flour.

5. Fill the cupcake liners two-thirds full. Bake until the sides of the cupcakes look firm but their centers are still soft.

6. Remove from the oven and cool for 20 minutes. Remove the liners gently. Serve warm, topped with whipped cream or vanilla ice cream.

Black Bottom Cupcakes

24 round chocolate cookies
1 1/3 cups granulated sugar
1/3 cup vegetable oil
1 cup water
1 tablespoon white vinegar
1 teaspoon vanilla extract
1 1/2 cups all-purpose flour
1 teaspoon baking soda
1/2 teaspoon salt
One 8-ounce package cream
   cheese, at room temperature
1 large egg
1 cup mini chocolate chips

1. Preheat the oven to 325°F. Insert liners into a medium cupcake pan, or grease the pan. Place a chocolate cookie in the bottom of each liner or pan.

2. In a large bowl cream together 1 cup of the sugar, the oil, and the water until blended. Stir in the vinegar and vanilla.

3. In a separate medium bowl mix together flour, baking soda, and 1/4 teaspoon of the salt.

4. Add all the dry mixture to the wet mixture and beat until incorporated. Set aside.

5. In a medium bowl beat together the cream cheese, egg, and the remaining sugar and salt. Stir in the chocolate chips.

6. Fill cupcake liners or pan half full with chocolate batter. Top with a heaping tablespoon of the cream cheese mixture. Bake for 25–30 minutes or until the edges of the cupcakes are puffed but the centers look moist. Cool cupcakes in the pan.

Blueberry Cupcakes

¼ pound (1 stick) unsalted
   butter, at room temperature
1 cup granulated sugar
2 large eggs
1½ cups all-purpose flour
1 teaspoon baking powder
½ teaspoon salt
⅓ cup milk
2 teaspoons vanilla extract
1½ cups blueberries (fresh or
   frozen)

1. Preheat the oven to 350°F. Insert liners into a medium cupcake pan.

2. With an electric mixer on medium speed, cream the butter and sugar together in a large bowl until fluffy, about 3–5 minutes. Add the eggs to the creamed mixture and beat well.

3. In a separate bowl sift together the flour, baking powder, and salt.

4. Beat portions of the dry ingredients into the creamed mixture, alternating with the milk. Mix for 3 minutes. With a spatula, fold in the vanilla and blueberries.

5. Fill cupcake liners one-half to three-quarters full with batter. Bake for 20–25 minutes or until a toothpick inserted in the center of cupcakes comes out clean. Cool cupcakes in the pan.

BLUEBERRY RASPBERRY CUPCAKES: Use ¾ cup fresh or frozen blueberries and ¾ cup fresh or frozen raspberries instead of only blueberries.

CRANBERRY CUPCAKES: Substitute 1½ cups cranberries for the blueberries.

Brownie Cupcakes

⅔ cup (4 ounces) unsweetened
   chocolate
½ pound (2 sticks) unsalted
   butter, at room temperature
1¼ cups granulated sugar
1 cup flour
1 teaspoon vanilla extract
4 large eggs
¾ cup mini chocolate chips
1 cup chopped pecans

1. Preheat the oven to 325°F. Insert liners into a mini or medium cupcake pan.

2. Melt the chocolate and butter together in a saucepan. Transfer to a large bowl.

3. Add the sugar, flour, and vanilla and mix well. Add the eggs one at a time, beating well after each addition.

4. Add chocolate chips and pecans.

5. Fill cupcake liners three-quarters full with batter. Bake mini cupcakes about 10 minutes and medium-sized cupcakes about 20 minutes until a toothpick inserted in the center of cupcakes comes out clean. Cool cupcakes in the pan.

Caramel Apple Cupcakes

1 cup firmly packed light brown
    sugar
½ cup vegetable oil
2 teaspoons ground cinnamon
1 tablespoon vanilla extract
2 large eggs
2 cups all-purpose flour
1 tablespoon baking powder
½ teaspoon salt
2 medium-sized tart apples,
    peeled, cored, and chopped
    small

1. Preheat the oven to 350°F. Insert liners into a medium cupcake pan.

2. In a large bowl beat together the brown sugar, oil, cinnamon, and vanilla with an electric mixer on medium speed. Add the eggs one at a time. Beat for 1 minute after each addition.

3. In a separate bowl sift together the flour, baking powder, and salt.

4. Slowly add the dry mixture to the wet mixture. Beat until blended. Stir in the apples.

5. Fill the cupcake liners one-half to three-quarters full with batter. Bake for 20–25 minutes or until a toothpick inserted in the center of cupcakes comes out clean. Cool cupcakes in the pan.

Champagne Cupcakes

⅔ cup butter, at room
    temperature
1½ cups granulated sugar
2¾ cups all-purpose flour
3 teaspoons baking powder
1 teaspoon salt
¾ cup champagne
6 large egg whites, at room
    temperature

1. Preheat the oven to 350°F. Insert liners into a medium cupcake pan.

2. In a large bowl cream together the butter and sugar until light and fluffy, about 3–5 minutes.

3. In a separate medium bowl sift together the flour, baking powder, and salt.

4. Blend the dry ingredients into the creamed mixture alternately with champagne.

5. In a large clean bowl beat the egg whites on high speed until stiff peaks form. Fold one-third of the whites into the batter until blended, then fold in the remaining egg whites until well blended.

6. Fill the cupcake liners three-quarters full with batter. Bake for about 20 minutes or until a toothpick inserted in the center of cupcakes comes out clean. Cool cupcakes in the pan.

Cheesecake Cupcakes

2 tablespoons unsalted butter, melted

12 graham crackers, finely crushed

Two 8-ounce packages cream cheese, at room temperature

1 cup granulated sugar

4 teaspoons all-purpose flour

½ teaspoon vanilla extract

½ teaspoon almond extract

4 large egg whites

½ teaspoon cream of tartar

1. Preheat the oven to 350°F. Insert liners into a medium cupcake pan and lightly coat with cooking spray.

2. Combine the butter and graham crackers in a small bowl. Evenly sprinkle 1 heaping teaspoon of the mixture on the bottoms of the cupcake liners.

3. In a large bowl combine the cream cheese, sugar, flour, vanilla, and almond extract with an electric mixer on medium speed until smooth.

4. In a separate bowl combine the egg whites and cream of tartar. With clean beaters, mix on high speed until stiff peaks form.

5. Carefully fold the egg white mixture into the cream cheese mixture.

6. Carefully spoon the batter into the cupcake liners until three-quarters full. Bake for 20–25 minutes or until the edges of the cupcakes are puffed but the centers look moist. Cover and chill cupcakes in the pan in the refrigerator until you are ready to serve them.

Cherry Cordial Cupcakes

1⅓ cups all-purpose flour
1¼ cups granulated sugar
⅓ cup cocoa powder
½ teaspoon baking soda
⅛ teaspoon salt
¾ cup water
2 large eggs
1 teaspoon vanilla extract
6 tablespoons butter, melted
    and warm
One 8-ounce package
    cream cheese
One 21-ounce can cherry
    pie filling
2 tablespoons coffee liqueur
½ teaspoon rum or rum extract
½ cup (3 ounces) semisweet
    chocolate chips

1. Preheat the oven to 350°F. Insert liners into a medium cupcake pan.

2. Combine the flour, 1 cup of the sugar, cocoa powder, baking soda, and salt into a large bowl.

3. Add the water, 1 of the eggs, vanilla, and melted butter. Mix until combined. Then beat with an electric mixer on low speed for 30 seconds.

4. In a separate small bowl beat the cream cheese and the remaining egg and sugar until smooth. Stir in ⅓ cup of the fruit filling, coffee liqueur, rum, and chocolate chips. Chill for at least 15 minutes.

5. Fill the cupcake liners one-third full. Top with 1 tablespoon cream cheese mixture and 1 tablespoon remaining fruit filling. Spoon additional batter over fillings until cupcake liners are two-thirds full. Bake for about 20 minutes or until a toothpick inserted in the center of cupcakes comes out clean. Cool cupcakes in the pan.

Chocolate Beer Cupcakes

¾ cup vegetable oil
4 teaspoons white vinegar
1 teaspoon vanilla extract
3 cups all-purpose flour
2 cups granulated sugar
2 teaspoons baking soda
½ cup cocoa powder
1 teaspoon salt
One 12-ounce bottle beer
1½ cups water

1. Preheat the oven to 325°F. Insert liners into a medium cupcake pan.

2. In a large mixing bowl combine the oil, vinegar, and vanilla.

3. In a separate bowl combine the flour, sugar, baking soda, cocoa powder, and salt.

4. With a spoon, make a well in the center of the dry ingredients. Pour oil mixture into the well. Pour the beer and water over the mixture. Beat well with an electric mixer on medium speed.

5. Fill the cupcake liners three-quarters full. Bake for about 20 minutes or until a toothpick inserted in the center of cupcakes comes out clean. Cool cupcakes in the pan.

Chocolate Carrot Cupcakes

1½ cups grated carrots
¾ cup granulated sugar
½ cup vegetable oil
1 cup boiling water
1½ cups all-purpose flour
1½ teaspoons baking powder
½ teaspoon salt
1 teaspoon ground cinnamon
½ cup cocoa powder
½ cup (3 ounces) mini
    chocolate chips

1. Preheat the oven to 350°F. Insert liners into a medium cupcake pan.

2. In a large bowl combine the carrots, sugar, and oil. Mix well on medium speed. Pour the boiling water over the mixture.

3. In a separate bowl combine the flour, baking powder, salt, cinnamon, and cocoa powder.

4. Add the dry ingredients to the carrot mixture. Mix well. Fold in the chocolate chips.

5. Fill the cupcake liners three-quarters full. Bake for about 20 minutes or until a toothpick inserted in the center of cupcakes comes out clean. Cool cupcakes in the pan.

Chocolate Chip Cinnamon Cupcakes

2 tablespoons ground
    cinnamon
1⅓ cups plus 3 tablespoons
    granulated sugar
6 eggs, separated
½ teaspoon lemon juice
¾ cup matzo meal
¼ cup potato starch
¼ cup water
1½ cups (9 ounces) semisweet
    chocolate chips

1. Preheat the oven to 350°F. Insert liners into a medium cupcake pan.

2. Combine 1 tablespoon of the cinnamon and 3 tablespoons of the granulated sugar in a small bowl. Set aside.

3. With an electric mixer on medium speed, beat the egg yolks, remaining sugar, and lemon juice until creamy.

4. In a separate bowl combine the matzo meal, 1 tablespoon cinnamon, and potato starch.

5. Add the egg mixture and water to the dry ingredients. Mix well. Fold in the chocolate chips.

6. With clean beaters, beat the egg whites on high speed until stiff peaks form. Gently fold the egg whites into the batter.

7. Fill the cupcake liners one-half to three-quarters full. Sprinkle cinnamon-sugar mixture over the butter. Bake for 20–25 minutes or until a toothpick inserted in the center of cupcakes comes out clean. Cool cupcakes in the pan.

Chocolate Chip Cookie Cupcakes

THE TOPPING

½ cup brown sugar

1 large egg

⅛ teaspoon salt

1 cup (6 ounces) semisweet
    chocolate chips

½ cup chopped walnuts

½ teaspoon vanilla extract

THE CUPCAKES

½ cup (1 stick) butter, at room
    temperature

6 tablespoons granulated sugar

6 tablespoons brown sugar

½ teaspoon vanilla extract

1 egg, at room temperature

1 cup all-purpose flour

½ teaspoon baking soda

½ teaspoon salt

1. Make the topping: In a large bowl combine the brown sugar, egg, and salt. Beat with an electric mixer at high speed until thick, about 5 minutes. Stir in the chocolate chips, nuts, and vanilla extract.

2. Preheat the oven to 375°F. Insert liners into a medium cupcake pan.

3. Combine the butter, sugars, and vanilla in a small bowl. Beat with an electric mixer on medium speed until creamy. Add the egg and beat for 1 minute.

4. In a separate small bowl combine the flour, baking soda, and salt.

5. Gradually add the dry ingredients to the egg mixture and mix with a rubber spatula or a wooden spoon until fully integrated.

6. Fill the cupcake liners half full. Bake for 15 minutes. Remove from the oven. Turn up the oven temperature to 425°F. Spoon 2 tablespoons of topping over each cupcake. Return the pan to the oven. Bake for 10 more minutes. Cool cupcakes in the pan.

Chocolate Cupcakes

½ cup cocoa powder

⅔ cup boiling water

⅔ cup (4 ounces) bittersweet chocolate, coarsely chopped

¼ pound plus 4 tablespoons (1½ sticks) unsalted butter, at room temperature

1½ cups granulated sugar

4 large eggs, at room temperature

1 teaspoon vanilla extract

2 cups all-purpose flour

1 teaspoon baking soda

¼ teaspoon salt

1 cup plain yogurt, at room temperature

1. Preheat the oven to 350°F. Insert liners into a medium cupcake pan.

2. Place the cocoa in a small bowl. Pour the boiling water over cocoa and whisk until all lumps are dissolved. Add the bittersweet chocolate to the cocoa paste, and stir until melted and smooth. Set aside to cool.

3. In a large bowl cream together the butter and sugar with an electric mixer on medium speed until fluffy, 3–5 minutes. Add the eggs one at a time and beat 1 minute after each addition. Add the vanilla.

4. In a separate bowl combine the flour, baking soda, and salt.

5. Add half of the dry ingredients to the butter mixture. Mix at low speed until well integrated. Add the yogurt and mix well. Add the remainder of the dry ingredients. Mix until combined. Add the chocolate. Mix until blended. Do not overmix.

6. Fill the cupcake liners one-half to three-quarters full. Bake for 20–25 minutes or until a toothpick inserted in the center of cupcakes comes out clean. Cool cupcakes in the pan.

CHOCOLATE CHOCOLATE CHIP CUPCAKES: Add 1½ cups of semi-sweet chocolate chips to the batter once mixed.

Chocolate Macaroon Cupcakes

2 tablespoons (1 ounce) bittersweet chocolate, chopped
¾ cup condensed milk
⅛ teaspoon salt
2 cups shredded coconut
1 teaspoon vanilla extract

1. Preheat the oven to 350°F. Lightly grease cupcake pans.

2. In a double boiler melt the chocolate with the condensed milk and salt. Stir in the shredded coconut and vanilla.

3. Fill the greased pans half full. Bake for about 30 minutes or until golden brown. Cool cupcakes in the pan.

Chocolate Raspberry Cupcakes

⅔ cup unsalted butter, at room temperature
1½ cups granulated sugar
2 large eggs
1 teaspoon almond extract
2 cups (16 ounces) sour cream
1⅓ cups all-purpose flour
¾ cup cocoa powder
2 teaspoons ground cinnamon
½ teaspoon baking soda
1 teaspoon salt
½ cup finely ground almonds, toasted
¾ cup raspberry preserves

1. Preheat the oven to 350°F. Insert liners into a medium cupcake pan.

2. In a large bowl cream the butter and sugar with an electric mixer on medium speed until fluffy, 3–5 minutes. Add the eggs to creamed mixture, mixing 1 minute after each addition. Add the almond extract and the sour cream.

3. In a separate bowl combine the flour, cocoa, cinnamon, baking soda, and salt. Add the ground almonds.

4. With the mixer on low speed, add the dry ingredients to the creamed mixture. Mix until completely integrated.

5. Fill the liners one-half to three-quarters full. Drop a teaspoon of raspberry preserves into each cup. Bake for 20–25 minutes or until a toothpick inserted in the center of cupcakes comes out clean. Cool cupcakes in the pan.

Coffee Cupcakes

12 large egg whites, cold
3 tablespoons espresso, at room temperature
1 tablespoon lemon juice
1 teaspoon cream of tartar
1 teaspoon vanilla extract
½ teaspoon almond extract
1½ cups granulated sugar
1 cup all-purpose flour
1 tablespoon ground espresso beans
½ teaspoon salt

1. Preheat the oven to 325°F. Insert liners into a medium cupcake pan.

2. In a large bowl combine the egg whites, espresso, lemon juice, cream of tartar, vanilla, and almond extract. With an electric mixer on high speed, beat until mixture is foamy with tiny bubbles, 2–3 minutes. Gradually add ¾ cup of the sugar until the foam is creamy white. Do not overbeat.

3. In a separate bowl combine ¾ cup sugar, flour, ground espresso beans, and salt.

4. Fold the dry ingredients into the egg mixture. Gently mix with a rubber spatula or wooden spoon until completely integrated.

5. Fill the cupcake liners three-quarters full. Bake for 20–25 minutes or until a toothpick inserted in the center of cupcakes comes out clean. Cool cupcakes in the pan.

HAZELNUT COFFEE CUPCAKES: Substitute hazelnut flavored coffee for espresso. Fold in 1½ cups chopped hazelnuts after wet and dry ingredients are fully integrated.

JAVA CHIP CUPCAKES: Fold in 1½ cups chopped dark chocolate after wet and dry ingredients are fully integrated.

Cookies and Cream Cupcakes

¼ pound (1 stick) unsalted
    butter, at room temperature
1 cup milk
2 teaspoons vanilla extract
2¼ cups all-purpose flour
1 tablespoon baking powder
½ teaspoon salt
1⅔ cups granulated sugar
3 large egg whites, at room
    temperature
1 cup chocolate sandwich
    cookies (about 10), lightly
    crushed

1. Preheat the oven to 350°F. Insert liners into a medium cupcake pan.

2. In a large bowl cream together the butter, milk, and vanilla with an electric mixer until fluffy, about 3–5 minutes.

3. In a separate bowl mix together the flour, baking powder, and salt.

4. Add the dry ingredients to butter mixture. Mix until integrated. Stir in the sugar. With an electric mixer on low speed, beat for 30 seconds. Turn the mixer up to medium speed and beat for 2 minutes. Add the egg whites. Beat for 2 more minutes. Stir in the crushed cookies.

5. Fill the cupcake liners three-quarters full. Bake for about 20 minutes or until a toothpick inserted in the center of cupcakes comes out clean. Cool cupcakes in the pan.

Corn Cupcakes

¼ cup brown sugar, plus more
    for sprinkling on top
¾ cup cornmeal
1¼ cups all-purpose flour
2 teaspoons baking powder
¼ cup unsalted butter, melted
    and cooled slightly
¼ cup honey
1 large egg
1 cup milk

1. Preheat the oven to 400°F. Insert liners into a medium cupcake pan.

2. Combine the brown sugar, cornmeal, flour, and baking powder in a large bowl. Add the melted butter, honey, egg, and milk. Stir until just moistened.

3. Fill the cupcake liners three-quarters full. Sprinkle the batter with brown sugar. Bake for about 15–20 minutes or until a toothpick inserted in the center of cupcakes comes out clean. Cool cupcakes in the pan.

Cream-Filled Cupcakes

1 cup brown sugar

1 cup milk

4 large egg yolks, separated into 2 bowls, at room temperature

10 tablespoons (5 ounces) unsweetened chocolate, chopped small

¼ pound (1 stick) unsalted butter, at room temperature

1 cup granulated sugar

2 cups all-purpose flour

1 teaspoon baking powder

1 teaspoon salt

¼ cup whipping cream

1 teaspoon vanilla extract

3 large egg whites, at room temperature

1. Preheat the oven to 325°F. Insert liners into a medium cupcake pan.

2. In a small bowl combine the brown sugar, ½ cup of the milk, and two of the egg yolks.

3. In a double boiler melt the chocolate. Add the brown sugar mixture to the melted chocolate, stirring constantly. When the mixture is shiny and thick, after about 3 minutes, set aside to cool.

4. In a clean large bowl cream together the butter and sugar with an electric mixer on medium speed until light and fluffy, about 3–5 minutes. Add remaining two egg yolks. Beat until combined. Pour the cooled chocolate mixture into the creamed butter and sugar. Beat until smooth.

5. In a separate bowl combine the flour, baking powder, and salt. Add the whipping cream, remaining ½ cup of milk, and vanilla. Mix with a rubber spatula or wooden spoon until combined.

6. Add the flour mixture to the batter. Beat well.

7. With clean beaters and a small bowl, beat the egg whites on high speed until soft peaks form. Gently fold the egg whites into the batter with rubber spatula.

8. Fill the cupcake liners three-quarters full. Bake for 20–25 minutes or until a toothpick inserted in the center of cupcakes comes out clean. Cool cupcakes in the pan.

9. When cool, remove with a grapefruit spoon a two-inch cake cone from the center of the cupcake. Spoon in pastry cream and replace cake cone. Frost

Eggnog Cupcakes

¾ pound (3 sticks) unsalted
    butter, at room temperature
2 cups granulated sugar
4 large eggs
1 teaspoon rum
1 teaspoon vanilla extract
1 teaspoon almond extract
3 cups all-purpose flour
1 teaspoon baking powder
¼ teaspoon ground nutmeg
½ teaspoon ground cinnamon
½ teaspoon salt
1 cup eggnog
Rum Syrup (page 100)

1. Preheat the oven to 350°F. Insert liners into a medium cupcake pan.

2. In a large bowl cream together the butter and sugar with an electric mixer on medium speed until fluffy, 3–5 minutes. Add the eggs one at a time. Beat well. Add the rum, vanilla, and almond extract. Mix well.

3. In a separate bowl mix together the flour, baking powder, nutmeg, cinnamon, and salt.

4. Add portions of the dry ingredients to the creamed mixture, alternating with portions of the eggnog. Mix for 3 minutes.

5. Fill the cupcake liners three-quarters full. Bake for 15–20 minutes or until a toothpick inserted in the center of cupcakes comes out clean. While the cupcakes are still warm, top with Rum Syrup (see page 100).

ROOTBEER CUPCAKES: Omit rum, eggnog, almond extract, nutmeg, cinnamon, and Rum Syrup. Add 1 cup root beer and ⅓ cup crushed root beer–flavored candies to the batter.

German Chocolate Cupcakes

⅔ cup (4 ounces) German
    sweet chocolate, coarsely
    chopped
12 tablespoons (1½ sticks)
    unsalted butter
1½ cups granulated sugar
3 large eggs
1 teaspoon vanilla extract
2 cups all-purpose flour
1 teaspoon baking soda
¼ teaspoon salt
1 cup milk

1. Preheat the oven to 350°F. Insert liners into a medium cupcake pan.

2. In a double boiler or microwave (using a microwave-safe bowl), melt the chocolate and butter together. Cool slightly. Stir the sugar into melted chocolate and butter mixture until blended. Add the eggs to mixture one at a time, beating with an electric mixer on medium speed after each addition. Add the vanilla. Mix.

3. In a separate large bowl sift together the flour, baking soda, and salt.

4. Add portions of the dry ingredients to creamed mixture, alternating with portions of the milk. Mix until completely integrated.

5. Fill cupcake liners three-quarters full. Bake for 20–25 minutes or until a toothpick inserted in the center of cupcakes comes out clean. Cool cupcakes in the pan.

Gingerbread Cupcakes

¼ pound (1 stick) unsalted
    butter, at room temperature
¼ cup dark brown sugar
¼ cup granulated sugar
1 large egg
⅔ cup light molasses
2 teaspoons lemon zest
2½ cups all-purpose flour
1½ teaspoons baking soda
1 teaspoon ground cinnamon
1¼ teaspoons ground ginger
½ teaspoon ground cloves
1 cup sour cream

1. Preheat the oven to 375°F. Insert liners into a medium cupcake pan.

2. In a large bowl cream the butter and sugars together with an electric mixer on medium speed until fluffy, 3–5 minutes. Add the egg, molasses, and lemon zest to creamed mixture. Beat well.

3. In a separate bowl combine the flour, baking soda, cinnamon, ginger, and cloves.

4. Add portions of the dry ingredients to the creamed mixture, alternating with portions of the sour cream, until they are completely integrated, about 30 seconds.

5. Fill the cupcake liners one-half to three-quarters full. Bake for 15–20 minutes or until a toothpick inserted in the center of cupcakes comes out clean. Cool cupcakes in the pan.

Golden Cupcakes

½ pound (2 sticks) unsalted
    butter, at room temperature
2 cups granulated sugar
4 large eggs, separated, at
    room temperature
2 teaspoons vanilla extract
3 cups all-purpose flour
4 teaspoons baking powder
½ teaspoon salt
1 cup milk

1. Preheat the oven to 350°F. Insert liners into a medium cupcake pan.

2. In a large bowl cream together the butter and sugar with an electric mixer on medium speed until fluffy, about 3–5 minutes. Add the egg yolks. Beat well. Add the vanilla. Mix.

3. In a separate bowl combine the flour, baking powder, and salt.

4. Add the dry ingredients to creamed mixture, alternating with the milk. Mix well.

5. With clean beaters, beat the egg whites on high speed until stiff peaks form. With a rubber spatula, gently fold the egg whites into the batter.

6. Fill the cupcake liners one-half to three-quarters full. Bake for 20–25 minutes or until a toothpick inserted in the center of cupcakes comes out clean. Cool cupcakes in the pan.

LICORICE CUPCAKES: Substitute 4 tablespoons licorice or anise flavoring for the vanilla extract.

Irish Cream Cupcakes

2/3 cup unsalted butter, at room
temperature
2 cups granulated sugar
2 large eggs, at room
temperature
2 teaspoons vanilla extract
1 1/3 cups Irish cream liqueur
2/3 cup milk
4 cups all-purpose flour
2 teaspoons baking powder
2 teaspoons salt

1. Preheat the oven to 325°F. Insert liners into a medium cupcake pan.

2. In a large bowl cream together the butter and sugar with an electric mixer on medium speed until fluffy, about 3–5 minutes. Add the eggs and vanilla. Beat well.

3. In a separate small bowl combine the liqueur and milk.

4. In another bowl combine the flour, baking powder, and salt.

5. Add the flour mixture to the creamed mixture, alternating with the liqueur mixture. Beat on medium speed for 2 minutes.

6. Fill the cupcake liners three-quarters full. Bake for about 20 minutes or until a toothpick inserted in the center of cupcakes comes out clean. Cool cupcakes in the pan.

Kahlúa Cupcakes

12 tablespoons (1 1/2 sticks)
unsalted butter, at room
temperature
1/2 cup cocoa powder
1 1/2 cups granulated sugar
1 tablespoon vanilla extract
3 large eggs, separated, at
room temperature
1/2 cup cold water
1/2 cup Kahlúa
2 1/4 cups all-purpose flour
3 teaspoons baking soda
1/2 teaspoon salt

1. Preheat the oven to 350°F. Insert liners into a medium cupcake pan.

2. In a large bowl cream together the butter, cocoa, sugar, and vanilla with an electric mixer on medium speed until light and creamy, 3–5 minutes. Add egg yolks and beat for 4 minutes.

3. In a small bowl mix water and Kahlúa.

4. In another large bowl combine the flour, baking soda, and salt.

5. Add the dry ingredients to the creamed mixture, alternating with the Kahlúa mixture. Mix on medium speed until ingredients are completely combined.

6. With clean beaters and a large bowl, beat the egg whites on high speed until they form soft peaks. Gradually beat in the remaining sugar to make a meringue. With a rubber spatula, fold the meringue into the batter.

7. Fill the cupcake liners three-quarters full. Bake for 20–25 minutes or until a toothpick inserted in the center of cupcakes comes out clean. Cool cupcakes in the pan.

Lemon Cupcakes

½ pound (2 sticks) unsalted
    butter, at room temperature
2 cups granulated sugar
4 large eggs, at room
    temperature
3 cups all-purpose flour
½ teaspoon baking soda
½ teaspoon salt
1 cup milk
2 tablespoons lemon zest
2 tablespoons fresh lemon juice
    or lemon concentrate

1. Preheat the oven to 325°F. Insert liners into a medium cupcake pan.

2. In a large bowl cream together the butter and sugar with an electric mixer on medium speed until fluffy, 3–5 minutes. Add the eggs one at a time to creamed mixture, beating 1 minute after each addition.

3. In a separate bowl combine the flour, baking soda, and salt.

4. Add the dry ingredients to the creamed mixture, alternating with the milk. Mix until completely integrated. Add the lemon zest and lemon juice. Mix the batter for 30 seconds.

5. Fill the cupcake liners three-quarters full. Bake for about 20 minutes or until a toothpick inserted in the center of cupcakes comes out clean. Cool cupcakes in the pan.

LEMON GINGER POPPY SEED CUPCAKES: Add 1 teaspoon ground ginger to the flour mixture. Add ¼ cup poppy seeds after you add the lemon zest and juice and mix gently.

LIME CUPCAKES: Substitute 1 cup sour cream for 1 cup milk, lime zest for lemon zest, and fresh lime juice or lime concentrate for lemon juice or lemon concentrate.

Low-Fat Carrot Cupcakes

1½ cups all-purpose flour
1 teaspoon baking soda
1 tablespoon baking powder
1 teaspoon ground cinnamon
¼ teaspoon ground nutmeg
¼ teaspoon ground ginger
1 large egg
2 tablespoons vegetable oil
¼ cup raisins
¼ cup chopped walnuts
½ cup low-fat milk
One 8-ounce can crushed
    pineapple
1½ cups grated carrots
¼ cup brown sugar

1. Preheat the oven to 350°F. Insert liners into a medium cupcake pan.

2. Combine the flour, baking soda, baking powder, cinnamon, nutmeg, and ginger in a large bowl. Mix well.

3. In a separate bowl combine the remaining ingredients. Stir until combined.

4. Add the wet ingredients to the dry ingredients. Stir to blend.

5. Fill the cupcake liners three-quarters full. Bake for 20–25 minutes or until a toothpick inserted in the center of cupcakes comes out clean. Cool cupcakes in the pan.

Low-Fat Chocolate Cupcakes

1½ cups all-purpose flour
¾ cup granulated sugar
¼ cup cocoa powder
2 teaspoons baking powder
1 teaspoon baking soda
½ teaspoon salt
⅔ cup vanilla yogurt
⅔ cup skim milk
½ teaspoon vanilla extract
1 cup (6 ounces) chocolate chips

1. Preheat the oven to 350°F. Insert liners into a medium cupcake pan.

2. Combine the flour, sugar, cocoa, baking powder, baking soda, and salt. Add the yogurt, milk, and vanilla. Mix until just combined. Fold in the chocolate chips.

3. Fill the cupcake liners three-quarters full. Bake for 15–20 minutes or until a toothpick inserted in the center of cupcakes comes out clean. Cool cupcakes in the pan.

Low-Fat White Cupcakes

4 tablespoons (½ stick) butter,
  at room temperature
1 cup granulated sugar
1 cup skim milk
2 tablespoons nonfat dry milk
1 large egg, at room
  temperature
2 teaspoons vanilla extract
1 teaspoon almond extract
2 cups all-purpose flour
2 teaspoons baking powder
⅛ teaspoon salt

1. Preheat the oven to 350°F. Insert liners into a medium cupcake pan and coat the liners with canola oil spray.

2. In a large bowl combine the butter and sugar with an electric mixer on low speed until coarse, about 1½ minutes.

3. In a small bowl beat the milk, dry milk, egg, vanilla, and almond extract. Add the milk mixture to the butter mixture and beat on medium speed until frothy, about 1 minute.

4. In a separate bowl combine the flour, baking powder, and salt. Make a well in the center of the dry ingredients. Pour the butter mixture into the well. Stir until fully combined. Beat with the electric mixer on medium speed for 10 seconds.

5. Fill the cupcake liners three-quarters full. Bake for about 20 minutes or until cupcakes are lightly browned and a toothpick inserted in the center of cupcakes comes out clean. Cool cupcakes in the pan.

Maple Walnut Cupcakes

¾ cup (1½ sticks) unsalted
  butter, at room temperature
½ cup granulated sugar
½ cup maple syrup
1 teaspoon vanilla extract
3 large eggs
2 cups all-purpose flour
2½ teaspoons baking powder
1 teaspoon salt
¼ cup milk
½ cup chopped walnuts

1. Preheat the oven to 350°F. Insert liners into a medium cupcake pan.

2. In a large bowl cream together the butter and sugar with an electric mixer on medium speed until fluffy, 3–5 minutes. Beat in the maple syrup. Add the vanilla and eggs. Beat until mixture is smooth.

3. In a separate bowl combine the flour, baking powder, and salt.

4. Add the flour mixture to the creamed mixture, alternating with the milk. Beat well. Stir in the walnuts.

5. Fill the cupcake liners three-quarters full. Bake for about 20 minutes or until a toothpick inserted in the center of cupcakes comes out clean. Cool cupcakes in the pan.

Mint Chocolate Chip Cupcakes

¼ cup (½ stick) unsalted butter, at room temperature

¾ cup granulated sugar

⅓ cup (2 ounces) unsweetened chocolate, coarsely chopped, melted

2 large eggs, at room temperature

1 teaspoon peppermint extract

½ cup chocolate milk

1½ cups all-purpose flour

1 teaspoon baking soda

½ cup (6 ounces) mini chocolate chips

1. Preheat the oven to 350°F. Insert liners into a medium cupcake pan.

2. In a large bowl cream together the butter and sugar with an electric mixer on medium speed until light and fluffy, 3–5 minutes. Beat the melted chocolate into the butter mixture. Add the eggs, peppermint extract, and chocolate milk. Beat until creamy.

3. In a separate medium-sized bowl combine the flour and baking soda.

4. Add the dry ingredients to the chocolate mixture and beat until well blended. With a rubber spatula, stir in the chocolate chips.

5. Fill the cupcake liners three-quarters full. Bake for 15–20 minutes or until a toothpick inserted in the center of cupcakes comes out clean. Cool cupcakes in the pan.

Mocha Cupcakes

2 cups granulated sugar

⅔ cup unsalted butter, at room temperature

2 large eggs, at room temperature

1 cup sour cream

2 cups all-purpose flour

1 teaspoon baking soda

5 tablespoons cocoa powder

3 tablespoons ground coffee

1 teaspoon salt

¾ cup strong black coffee

2 teaspoons vanilla extract

1. Preheat the oven to 350°F. Insert liners into a medium cupcake pan.

2. In a large bowl cream together the sugar, butter, and eggs with an electric mixer on medium speed until fluffy, 3–5 minutes. Mix in the sour cream.

3. In a separate bowl mix together the flour, baking soda, cocoa, ground coffee, and salt.

4. In a measuring cup combine the coffee and vanilla.

5. Add the dry ingredients to the creamed mixture, alternating with the coffee mixture. Mix thoroughly.

6. Fill the cupcake liners three-quarters full. Bake for 20–25 minutes or until a toothpick inserted in the center of cupcakes comes out clean. Cool cupcakes in the pan.

PEPPERMINT MOCHA CUPCAKES: Add 1 teaspoon peppermint extract and ¾ cup peppermint chips.

Mousse Cupcakes

6 eggs
¼ cup plus 2 tablespoons all-purpose flour
2⅓ cups (14 ounces) milk chocolate, coarsely chopped, melted, and cooled slightly
Whipped Cream

1. Preheat the oven to 325°F. Insert liners into mini or medium cupcake pans.

2. In a large bowl beat together the eggs and flour with an electric mixer on medium speed. Add the melted chocolate. Beat until combined.

3. Fill the cupcake liners three-quarters full. Bake mini cupcakes for 7–10 minutes and medium cupcakes for 12–15 minutes, or till the cakes are set but the centers still shake. Cool in the pan for 20 minutes. The centers will set into a mousse.

4. When cool, top with Whipped Cream (page 93). Peel paper liners off carefully and eat directly from the liner.

Oatmeal Raisin Cupcakes

¼ pound (1 stick) unsalted butter, at room temperature
½ cup granulated sugar
¾ cup firmly packed brown sugar, plus more for sprinkling on top
1 cup milk
1½ cups sifted all-purpose flour
1 cup quick-cooking oatmeal
1 teaspoon baking soda
½ teaspoon salt
½ teaspoon ground cinnamon
¼ teaspoon ground cloves
¼ teaspoon ground allspice
2 large eggs, at room temperature
⅔ cup raisins

1. Preheat the oven to 350°F. Insert liners into a medium cupcake pan.

2. In a large bowl cream together the butter, sugars, and ¾ cup of the milk with an electric mixer on medium speed.

3. In a separate bowl combine the flour, oatmeal, baking soda, salt, cinnamon, cloves, and allspice.

4. Add the dry ingredients to the creamed mixture. Beat at low speed for 30 seconds to combine the ingredients, then at high speed for 2 minutes. Add the remaining ¼ cup milk and the eggs. Continue to beat for 2 minutes. Fold in the raisins.

5. Fill the cupcake liners three-quarters full. Sprinkle with brown sugar. Bake for 20–25 minutes or until a toothpick inserted in the center of cupcakes comes out clean. Cool cupcakes in the pan.

Peanut Butter Cupcakes

6 tablespoons unsalted butter,
  at room temperature
1 cup smooth or crunchy
  peanut butter
1⅓ cups firmly packed
  brown sugar
3 large eggs
1 tablespoon vanilla extract
3 cups all-purpose flour
1 tablespoon baking powder
1 teaspoon salt
1 cup milk

1. Preheat the oven to 350°F. Insert liners into a medium cupcake pan.

2. In a large bowl cream together the butter, peanut butter, and brown sugar with an electric mixer on medium speed until fluffy, about 3–5 minutes. Add the eggs. Beat well. Mix in the vanilla.

3. In a separate bowl combine the flour, baking powder, and salt.

4. Add the dry ingredients to creamed mixture, alternating with the milk. Mix well.

5. Fill the cupcake liners one-half to three-quarters full. Bake for 15–20 minutes or until a toothpick inserted in the center of cupcakes comes out clean. Cool cupcakes in the pan.

Pecan Pie Cupcakes

½ pound (2 sticks) unsalted
    butter, at room temperature
2 cups granulated sugar
4 large eggs, separated, at
    room temperature
3 teaspoons vanilla extract
3 cups all-purpose flour
4 teaspoons baking powder
½ teaspoon salt
1 cup milk
2½ cups pecans
1½ cups light corn syrup
3 large eggs, at room
    temperature
½ cup firmly packed dark
    brown sugar

1. Preheat the oven to 350°F. Insert liners into a medium cupcake pan.

2. In a large bowl cream together the butter and sugar with an electric mixer on medium speed until fluffy, 3–5 minutes. Add 4 egg yolks. Beat well. Add 2 teaspoons of the vanilla. Mix.

3. In a separate bowl combine the flour, baking powder, and salt.

4. Add the dry ingredients to creamed mixture, alternating with the milk. Mix well.

5. With clean beaters and medium-sized bowl, beat 4 egg whites on high speed until stiff peaks form. Gently fold the whites into the batter with a spatula.

6. Fold in 1 cup of the pecans.

7. Reserve ⅔ cup batter. Fill the cupcake liners half full with batter. Bake for 5 minutes.

8. Combine the reserved batter with corn syrup, 3 eggs, brown sugar, the remaining 1 teaspoon of vanilla, and the remaining 1½ cups of pecans.

9. Spoon the pecan topping on partially baked cupcakes.

10. Bake for 15–20 minutes or until a toothpick inserted in the center of cupcakes comes out clean. Cool cupcakes in the pan.

Peppermint Cupcakes

½ pound (2 sticks) unsalted
    butter, at room temperature
2 cups granulated sugar
4 large eggs, at room
    temperature
1 tablespoon peppermint
    extract
3 cups all-purpose flour
1 teaspoon baking soda
½ teaspoon salt
1 cup milk
½ cup ground peppermint
    candies
½ cup boiling water

1. Preheat the oven to 300°F. Insert liners into a medium cupcake pan.

2. In a large bowl cream together the butter and sugar with an electric mixer on medium speed until fluffy, 3–5 minutes.

3. In a separate bowl, with clean beaters on medium speed, beat the eggs and peppermint extract together.

4. Add the egg mixture to the creamed mixture.

5. In a separate bowl combine the flour, baking soda, and salt.

6. Gradually add the dry ingredients to the creamed mixture, alternating with the milk. Do not overmix. Sprinkle the ground peppermint candies into the batter. Add the boiling water and partially melt the candies. Mix slightly.

7. Fill the cupcake liners three-quarters full. Bake for about 20 minutes or until a toothpick inserted in the center of cupcakes comes out clean. Cool cupcakes in the pan.

Piña Colada Cupcakes

¼ pound (1 stick) unsalted but-
    ter, melted and cooled
⅓ cup pineapple juice
1 tablespoon rum
2 teaspoons vanilla extract
3 large eggs
1½ cups all-purpose flour
1 cup granulated sugar
1 teaspoon baking powder
½ teaspoon baking soda
¼ teaspoon salt
⅓ cup crushed pineapple
⅓ cup shredded coconut

1. Preheat the oven to 350°F. Insert liners into a medium cupcake pan.

2. In a large bowl beat together the melted butter, pineapple juice, rum, and vanilla with an electric mixer at medium speed until light and fluffy. Add the eggs one at a time, mixing well after each addition.

3. In a separate bowl combine the flour, sugar, baking powder, baking soda, and salt.

4. With the mixer on low speed, add the dry ingredients to the creamed mixture ½ cup at a time until combined. Fold in the pineapple and coconut.

5. Fill the cupcake liners three-quarters full. Bake for 20–25 minutes or until a toothpick inserted in the center of cupcakes comes out clean. Cool cupcakes in the pan.

Pumpkin Cupcakes

¼ pound (1 stick) unsalted
    butter, at room temperature
1 cup firmly packed dark brown
    sugar
⅓ cup granulated sugar
2 large eggs, at room
    temperature
2 cups all-purpose flour
2 teaspoons baking powder
¼ teaspoon baking soda
1 teaspoon ground cinnamon
1 teaspoon ground ginger
½ teaspoon ground nutmeg
⅛ teaspoon ground cloves
½ teaspoon salt
½ cup milk
1¼ cups pumpkin puree,
    canned or fresh
1 teaspoon vanilla extract

1. Preheat the oven to 350°F. Insert liners into a medium cupcake pan.

2. In a large bowl cream together the butter and sugars with an electric mixer on medium speed until fluffy, 3–5 minutes. Add the eggs to the creamed mixture one at a time, mixing after each addition. Beat well.

3. In a separate bowl combine the flour, baking powder, baking soda, cinnamon, ginger, nutmeg, cloves, and salt.

4. Add the dry ingredients to the creamed mixture, alternating with milk. Mix until completely integrated.

5. Add the pumpkin and vanilla and beat until smooth.

6. Fill the cupcake liners one-half to three-quarters full. Bake for 20–25 minutes or until a toothpick inserted in the center of cupcakes comes out clean. Cool cupcakes in the pan.

Rich Chocolate Cupcakes

¼ pound (1 stick) unsalted
   butter, at room temperature
½ cup (3 ounces) unsweetened
   chocolate, coarsely chopped
1 cup boiling water
1 teaspoon vanilla extract
2 cups granulated sugar
½ cup sour cream
2 cups all-purpose flour
1 teaspoon baking powder
1 teaspoon baking soda
2 large egg whites, at room
   temperature

1. Preheat the oven to 325°F. Insert liners into mini or medium cupcake pans.

2. Place the butter and chocolate in a large bowl. Pour the boiling water over them, and let stand until melted. Stir to combine. Stir in the vanilla and sugar.

3. Add the sour cream and mix on medium speed until fully integrated.

4. In a separate bowl combine the flour, baking powder, and baking soda.

5. Gradually add the dry ingredients to the batter, mixing at medium speed until smooth.

6. In another bowl with clean beaters, whip the egg whites until stiff. Gently fold the egg whites into the batter.

7. Fill the cupcake liners three-quarters full. Bake mini cupcakes 10–15 minutes and medium cupcakes 20–25 minutes, or until a toothpick inserted in the center of cupcakes comes out clean. Cool cupcakes in the pan.

Sea Breeze Cupcakes

¼ pound (1 stick) unsalted
  butter, at room temperature
¾ cup granulated sugar
2 large eggs, separated, at
  room temperature
1½ cups all-purpose flour
1½ teaspoons baking powder
¼ teaspoon baking soda
¼ teaspoon salt
¼ cup pink grapefruit juice
¼ cup cranberry juice
Zest of 1 small grapefruit
¾ cup chopped cranberries

1. Preheat the oven to 350°F. Insert liners into a medium cupcake pan.

2. In a large bowl cream together the butter and sugar with an electric mixer on medium speed until fluffy, 3–5 minutes. Add the egg yolks. Beat well.

3. In a separate bowl combine the flour, baking powder, baking soda, and salt.

4. Add the dry ingredients to the creamed mixture, alternating with grapefruit and cranberry juices. Fold in the grapefruit zest and chopped cranberries.

5. With clean beaters, whip the egg whites until stiff peaks form. Gently fold the whites with a rubber spatula into the batter.

6. Fill the cupcake liners one-half to two-thirds full. Bake for 20–25 minutes or until a toothpick inserted in the center of cupcakes comes out clean. Cool cupcakes in the pan.

ORANGE CUPCAKES: Substitute ½ cup orange juice for pink grapefruit and cranberry juice. Substitute zest of 2 oranges for grapefruit zest, and omit cranberries.

Sour Cream Coffee Cake Cupcakes

½ cup (1 stick) butter, at room
temperature

1 cup granulated sugar

2 eggs, at room temperature

2 teaspoons vanilla extract

2 cups all-purpose flour

1¼ teaspoons baking powder

1 teaspoon baking soda

½ teaspoon salt

1 cup sour cream

1 cup chopped walnuts

1. Make Streusel Topping (see page 101).

2. Preheat the oven to 325°F. Insert liners into a medium cupcake pan.

3. In a large bowl cream together the butter and sugar with an electric mixer at medium speed until fluffy, 3–5 minutes. Add the eggs one at a time, and beat about 1 minute after each addition. Blend in the vanilla.

4. In a separate bowl combine the flour, baking powder, baking soda, and salt.

5. Add the dry ingredients to creamed mixture, alternating with the sour cream. Beat until smooth. Fold in the walnuts.

6. Fill the cupcake liners two-thirds full. Sprinkle the Streusel Topping over the cupcakes to the top of the liners. Bake for 20 minutes or until a toothpick inserted in the center of cupcakes comes out clean. Cool cupcakes in the pan.

Spice Cupcakes   *very good!*

½ cup molasses

½ cup boiling water

¼ cup (½ stick) unsalted butter,
at room temperature

¼ cup granulated sugar

1 large egg, at room
temperature

1⅓ cups all-purpose flour

1 teaspoon baking soda

1½ teaspoons ground cinnamon

½ teaspoon ground nutmeg

¼ teaspoon ground cloves

½ teaspoon salt

1. Preheat the oven to 350°F. Insert liners into a medium cupcake pan.

2. In a small bowl combine the molasses and boiling water. Set aside.

3. In a large bowl cream together the butter and sugar with an electric mixer on medium speed until fluffy, 3–5 minutes. Add the egg to the creamed mixture. Beat well.

4. In a separate bowl combine the remaining ingredients.

5. Beat the flour mixture into the creamed mixture, alternating with the molasses mixture. Beat well after each addition.

6. Fill the cupcake liners three-quarters full. Bake for about 15–20 minutes or until a toothpick inserted in the center of cupcakes comes out clean. Cool cupcakes in the pan.

makes 1 dozen

Strawberry Cupcakes

¼ pound (1 stick) unsalted
    butter, at room temperature
1 cup granulated sugar
2 large eggs
1½ cups all-purpose flour
1 teaspoon baking powder
½ teaspoon salt
⅓ cup milk
1 teaspoon vanilla extract
1½ cups fresh or frozen
    strawberries, sliced

1. Preheat the oven to 350°F. Insert liners into a medium cupcake pan.

2. In a large bowl cream together the butter and sugar with an electric mixer on medium speed until fluffy, 3–5 minutes. Add the eggs one at a time. Beat well after each addition.

3. In a separate bowl combine the flour, baking powder, and salt.

4. Add the dry ingredients to the creamed mixture, alternating with the milk. Mix for 3 minutes. With a rubber spatula, fold in the vanilla and strawberries.

5. Fill the cupcake liners one-half to three-quarters full. Bake for 20–25 minutes or until a toothpick inserted in the center of cupcakes comes out clean. Cool cupcakes in the pan.

STRAWBERRY LIME CUPCAKES: Fold in 2 teaspoons lime juice and 1 teaspoon grated lime zest along with the vanilla and strawberries.

Tres Leches Cupcakes

½ cup (1 stick) unsalted butter,
    at room temperature
1 cup granulated sugar
5 large eggs, at room
    temperature
½ teaspoon vanilla extract
1½ cups all-purpose flour
1 teaspoon baking powder
1 cup whole milk
¾ cup plus 2 tablespoons
    (7 ounces) sweetened
    condensed milk
¾ cup (6 ounces) evaporated
    milk
⅓ cup liqueur (Frangelico,
    brandy, or Chambord),
    optional

1. Preheat the oven to 350°F. Insert liners into a medium cupcake pan.

2. In a large bowl cream together the butter and sugar with an electric mixer on medium speed until fluffy, 3–5 minutes. Add the eggs and vanilla. Beat well.

3. In a separate bowl sift together the flour and baking powder. Add the flour mixture to the butter mixture. Mix until blended.

4. Fill the cupcake liners three-quarters full. Bake for 20–25 minutes or until a toothpick inserted in the center of cupcakes comes out clean. Cool cupcakes in the pan.

5. Combine the whole milk, condensed milk, evaporated milk, and liqueur. Pierce the cooled cupcakes with a fork, and with a spoon pour the milk mixture over the tops of the cupcakes. Refrigerate for at least 2 hours before serving. Top with whipped cream.

Vegan Chocolate Cupcakes

6 tablespoons applesauce
2¼ cups water
1 teaspoon vanilla extract
2 tablespoons white vinegar
2½ cups unbleached
    all-purpose flour
⅔ cup cocoa powder
2 cups unbleached cane sugar
½ teaspoon salt
2 teaspoons baking soda

1. Preheat the oven to 375°F. Insert liners into a medium cupcake pan.

2. In a large bowl mix together the applesauce, water, vanilla, and vinegar.

3. In a separate bowl mix together the remaining ingredients.

4. Gradually add the dry ingredients to the liquid mixture. Beat well.

5. Fill the cupcake liners three-quarters full. Bake for 20–25 minutes or until a toothpick in the center of cupcakes comes out clean. Cool cupcakes in the pan.

Vegan White Cupcakes

½ cup vegan margarine, at
    room temperature
1⅓ cups unbleached cane sugar
3 cups unbleached all-purpose
    flour
¾ teaspoon salt
1 teaspoon baking powder
2 cups soy or rice milk
1 tablespoon vanilla extract
1 teaspoon almond extract

1. Preheat the oven to 350°F. Insert liners into a medium cupcake pan.

2. In a large bowl cream together the margarine and sugar with an electric mixer on medium speed until light and fluffy, 3–5 minutes.

3. In a separate bowl combine the flour, salt, and baking powder.

4. Add the dry ingredients to the creamed mixture, alternating with the soy or rice milk. Add the vanilla and almond extract and beat for 2 minutes at medium speed.

5. Fill the cupcake liners three-quarters full. Bake for about 20 minutes or until a toothpick inserted in the center of cupcakes comes out clean. Cool cupcakes in the pan.

White Chocolate Cupcakes

⅔ cup milk
1 tablespoon white vinegar
⅔ cup unsalted butter, at room
    temperature
1⅓ cup granulated sugar
3 large eggs, at room
    temperature
1¼ cups white chocolate chips
⅓ cup water
1 teaspoon vanilla extract
2 cups all-purpose flour
¾ teaspoon baking soda
¼ teaspoon salt

1. Preheat the oven to 325°F. Insert liners into a medium cupcake pan.

2. Combine the milk and vinegar in a cup. Set aside for at least 5 minutes.

3. In a large bowl cream together the butter and sugar with an electric mixer on medium speed until light and fluffy, 3–5 minutes. Add the eggs one at a time, beating after each addition.

4. Combine ½ cup of the white chocolate chips and the water in a small saucepan. Heat over low heat until melted, stirring continuously.

5. Add the vanilla and white chocolate mixture to the creamed mixture.

6. In a separate bowl combine the flour, baking soda, and salt.

7. Add the dry ingredients to the creamed mixture, alternating with the milk-and-vinegar mixture, beating for 1 minute after each addition. Fold in the remaining white chocolate chips.

8. Fill the cupcake liners three-quarters full. Bake for 20–25 minutes or until a toothpick inserted in the center of cupcakes comes out clean. Cool cupcakes in the pan.

White Cupcakes

½ cup (1 stick) unsalted butter, at room temperature
1 cup granulated sugar
2 large eggs, separated, at room temperature
1 teaspoon vanilla extract
1½ cups all-purpose flour
1½ teaspoons baking powder
¼ teaspoon salt
½ cup milk
⅛ teaspoon cream of tartar

1. Preheat the oven to 350°F. Insert liners into a medium cupcake pan.

2. In a large bowl beat the butter with an electric mixer on medium speed until soft, about 2 minutes. Add the sugar and beat until light and fluffy, about 3 minutes. Add the egg yolks one at a time, beating after each addition. Add the vanilla and beat until combined.

3. In a separate bowl combine the flour, baking powder, and salt.

4. With the mixer on low speed, alternately add the flour mixture and milk until combined.

5. In a small bowl with clean beaters beat the egg whites on high speed until foamy. Add the cream of tartar and continue beating until stiff peaks form. With a rubber spatula, stir a little of the whites into the batter to lighten it, then fold in the remaining whites until combined. Do not overmix.

6. Fill the cupcake liners three-quarters full. Bake for about 15–20 minutes or until a toothpick inserted in the center of cupcakes comes out clean. Cool cupcakes in the pan.

Zucchini Cupcakes

½ cup vegetable oil
1⅓ cups granulated sugar
3 large eggs
½ cup orange juice
1 teaspoon almond extract
2½ cups all-purpose flour
2 teaspoons baking powder
1 teaspoon baking soda
1 teaspoon salt
2 teaspoons ground cinnamon
½ teaspoon ground cloves
1½ cups shredded zucchini

1. Preheat the oven to 350°F. Insert liners into a medium cupcake pan.

2. In a large bowl combine the oil, sugar, eggs, orange juice, and almond extract. Beat well with an electric mixer.

3. In a separate bowl combine the flour, baking powder, baking soda, salt, cinnamon, and cloves.

4. Gradually add the dry ingredients to the wet mixture. Mix well.

5. Fold the zucchini into the batter.

6. Fill the cupcake liners three-quarters full. Bake for 20–25 minutes or until a toothpick inserted in the center of cupcakes comes out clean. Cool cupcakes in the pan.

Mother's Day and Father's Day Cupcakes

Part of the fun of Mother's Day and Father's Day is that parents get to take center stage and get a well-deserved break from the kitchen. Cupcakes loaded with fresh seasonal fruit are a great way to celebrate. These recipes use cake mixes and store-bought icing, so they are super easy for kids to make (with just a little help from Mom or Dad).

STRAWBERRY SHORTCAKE CUPCAKES

You will need:

Yellow cake mix
Fresh strawberries
Whipped cream
Red coloredsugar

Bake yellow cake mix cupcakes according to the instructions on the box. Slice the strawberries and place on the cupcakes tops. Spoon or squirt on prepared whipped cream. Sprinkle with red sugar. Place a whole strawberry in the center of each cupcake.

BLACKBERRY CUPCAKES

You will need:

White cake mix
1 cup blackberries, plus extra for decorating
Vanilla Frosting recipe (page 92)
Purple colored sugar
White nonpareils

Prepare cupcakes pans. Make cupcakes according to box directions, adding 1 cup of blackberries to the cake batter before baking. Bake and cool cupcakes. Frost the cupcakes. Sprinkle cupcakes with purple sugar. Spread a mound of white frosting in the center of the cupcake tops. Sprinkle with white nonpareils. Place blackberries around the white frosting in circular patterns.

CHOCOLATE CHERRY CUPCAKES

You will need:

Chocolate cake mix
Fresh cherries
Chocolate Frosting recipe (page 84)
Chocolate and red sprinkles
Chocolate-covered cherries (page 39)

Prepare cupcakes pans. Make chocolate cupcakes according to box directions, adding one cup of pitted cherries to the cake batter before baking. Bake, cool, and frost the cupcakes. Combine the sprinkles in a small bowl. Dip the edges of the frosted cupcakes into the sprinkles. Place chocolate-covered cherries on cupcake tops.

PEACHES AND CREAM CUPCAKES

You will need:

Yellow cake mix
Vanilla instant pudding
Whipped cream
Orange-colored sugar
Sliced peaches

Prepare the yellow cake mix cupcakes and vanilla instant pudding according to the instructions on the boxes. Place a tablespoon of vanilla pudding on the center of cupcake tops. Apply whipped cream around the cupcake perimeters. Sprinkle with orange sugar. Arrange sliced peaches in a pattern on cupcake tops.

FROSTING RECIPES

All frosting and icing recipes yield 2–2½ cups frosting.

Almond Frosting

3 cups confectioners' sugar
2 teaspoons almond extract
3 tablespoons hot water

1. Mix together the confectioners' sugar, almond extract, and hot water.

2. Beat to desired spreading consistency, adding more water or sugar as needed.

Banana Coconut Frosting

5 ½ tablespoons unsalted butter
1 cup coconut
⅔ cup finely chopped pecans
½ cup mashed bananas
1 teaspoon lemon juice
8 cups confectioners' sugar

1. Melt 2 tablespoons butter in a large skillet. Stir in coconut and pecans. Cook, stirring constantly, over medium heat until coconut and nuts are golden brown, about 8 minutes.

2. In a small bowl combine the bananas and lemon juice.

3. In a separate bowl cream the remaining butter with an electric mixer on medium speed. Add the sugar, then the banana mixture. Blend well. Add the coconut-pecan mixture. Mix well.

Browned Butter Icing

4 tablespoons (½ stick) unsalted butter
4 cups confectioners' sugar
1 teaspoon vanilla extract
⅛ teaspoon salt
¼ cup milk

1. Brown the butter in a small saucepan or a microwave.

2. Blend the sugar, vanilla, salt, and milk. Add browned butter and stir until smooth, adding a little milk or sugar as needed to reach desired spreading consistency.

Champagne Buttercream Icing

¾ cup vegetable shortening
12 tablespoons (1½ sticks)
   unsalted butter, at room
   temperature
3 tablespoons champagne
4½ cups confectioners' sugar

1. In a large bowl beat the shortening and butter until combined. Add the champagne. Slowly add the confectioners' sugar and beat until smooth. If necessary, add additional champagne to achieve desired spreading consistency.

Chocolate Frosting

6 tablespoons butter
2 teaspoons vanilla extract
3 cups confectioners' sugar
¾ cup cocoa powder
⅓ cup milk

1. Cream the butter and vanilla together with an electric mixer on low to medium speed.

2. In a separate bowl, combine the confectioners' sugar and cocoa powder.

3. Add the dry ingredients to the creamed mixture until fully integrated. Slowly add the milk to the frosting until you have reached desired consistency. You might not use all of the milk. Beat with an electric mixer for 1 minute or until creamy.

Chocolate Ganache

1 cup (6 ounces) white or dark
   chocolate
¾ cup whipping cream

1. Place the chocolate in a bowl.

2. In a saucepan bring the whipping cream just to a boil over high heat.

3. Pour the hot whipping cream over the chocolate and stir until chocolate is melted. Let the ganache cool to room temperature.

Chocolate Macaroon Glaze

2 cups confectioners' sugar
¼ cup cocoa powder
1 tablespoon unsalted butter
½ teaspoon vanilla extract
3 tablespoons milk
¾ cup shredded coconut

1. In a medium bowl combine the sugar, cocoa powder, and butter. Add the vanilla, and stir to mix. Add the milk gradually to achieve desired consistency and stir until smooth. Fold in the coconut.

Coconut Pecan Frosting

One 12-ounce can evaporated milk
1 ½ cups granulated sugar
¾ cup (1 ½ sticks) unsalted butter
4 egg yolks
1 ½ teaspoons vanilla extract
2 ⅔ cups shredded coconut
1 ½ cups chopped pecans

1. Combine the evaporated milk, sugar, butter, egg yolks, and vanilla in a large saucepan. Stir constantly over medium heat for 12 minutes or until thickened and golden brown. Remove from heat.
2. Stir in the coconut and pecans.
3. Cool to room temperature until spreading consistency.

Coffee Cream Cheese Frosting

One 8-ounce package cream cheese, at room temperature
2 tablespoons evaporated milk
1 teaspoon vanilla extract
⅛ teaspoon salt
2 cups confectioners' sugar
4 teaspoons instant coffee grounds or ground espresso beans

1. In a medium bowl beat together the cream cheese and evaporated milk until smooth.
2. Add remaining ingredients and beat until desired spreading consistency is achieved.

Cream Cheese Frosting

One 8-ounce package cream
cheese, at room
temperature
6 tablespoons (¾ stick)
unsalted butter, at room
temperature
3 cups confectioners' sugar
1 teaspoon vanilla extract

1. In a medium bowl cream together the cream cheese and butter with an electric mixer on medium speed until smooth.

2. Slowly sift in the confectioners' sugar and continue beating. Mix until all lumps are gone. Add the vanilla and mix until fully integrated.

GINGER CREAM CHEESE FROSTING: Add ½ teaspoon ground ginger.

MAPLE CREAM CHEESE FROSTING: Add 3 tablespoons maple syrup.

PEPPERMINT CREAM CHEESE FROSTING: Add 2 teaspoons peppermint extract and ⅓ cup crushed peppermint candies.

Dark Chocolate Icing

1 pint heavy cream
1 cup granulated sugar
1 cup (6 ounces) unsweetened
dark chocolate, coarsely
chopped
¼ pound (1 stick) butter
1 tablespoon vanilla extract
Pinch salt

1. Bring the cream and sugar to a simmer in a saucepan over medium heat, stirring constantly. Turn heat to low and cook for 6 minutes. Remove from heat.

2. Stir in the chocolate and butter until melted.

3. Stir in the vanilla and salt.

4. Refrigerate until the icing reaches spreading consistency, about 30 minutes.

Fudge Frosting

¼ cup heavy or whipping cream
1 ½ teaspoons corn syrup
2 tablespoons granulated sugar
1 ½ tablespoons unsalted
butter
1 teaspoon vanilla extract
⅓ cup (2 ounces) semisweet
chocolate, coarsely chopped

1. Place the cream, corn syrup, and sugar into a small saucepan. Bring to a boil over high heat. Remove from heat.

2. Add the butter, vanilla, and chocolate to the pan, stirring until melted and smooth. Refrigerate until the frosting is at a spreadable consistency.

Irish Cream Frosting

1 pound confectioners' sugar
5 1/2 tablespoons unsalted
    butter, at room temperature
1/4 cup milk
1/4 teaspoon salt
3 tablespoons Irish cream
    liqueur

1. Place all the ingredients into a small bowl and beat until fluffy. Add Irish cream or confectioners' sugar as needed to reach desired consistency.

Lemon Icing

4 cups confectioners' sugar
1/4 pound (1 stick) unsalted
    butter
3 tablespoons lemon zest
1/2 cup lemon juice
Few drops of yellow food
    coloring, optional

1. In a large bowl cream together the sugar and butter with an electric mixer on medium speed until smooth. Mix in the lemon zest, lemon juice, and food coloring until spreading consistency is achieved.

LIME ICING: Substitute lime zest for lemon zest; lime juice for lemon juice; and green food coloring for yellow food coloring.

Liqueur Icing

3 cups confectioners' sugar
6 tablespoons heavy cream
3 tablespoons liqueur (rum,
    amaretto, or brandy)

1. Combine all the ingredients in a medium mixing bowl. Beat on low speed until smooth. Add additional liqueur or confectioners' sugar if necessary to reach desired spreading consistency.

Low-Fat Chocolate Frosting

1⅓ cups confectioners' sugar
⅓ cup cocoa powder
¼ cup fat-free sour cream
¼ cup skim milk
½ teaspoon vanilla extract

1. In a small bowl combine the confectioners' sugar and cocoa. Add the sour cream, milk, and vanilla. With an electric mixer on medium-low speed beat until thoroughly combined.

Low-Fat Cream Cheese Frosting

½ cup fat-free or light
   cream cheese, at room
   temperature
2½ cups confectioners' sugar
1 teaspoon lemon juice
¼ teaspoon vanilla extract

1. Beat together the cream cheese, confectioners' sugar, lemon juice, and vanilla until smooth. Beat in additional confectioners' sugar until desired consistency is reached.

Low-Fat 7-Minute Frosting

2 egg whites
1½ cups granulated sugar
1 tablespoon light corn syrup
⅓ cup cold water
2 teaspoons vanilla extract

1. Place all of the ingredients except the vanilla in a double boiler over boiling water. Beat constantly with an electric mixer on medium-high speed until stiff peaks form, 4–7 minutes. Remove from heat.

2. Add the vanilla. Beat to spreading consistency.

CITRUS LOW-FAT 7-MINUTE FROSTING: Replace the water with lemon, orange, or lime juice. Spoon in 1 tablespoon of zest.

COFFEE LOW-FAT 7-MINUTE FROSTING: Replace the granulated sugar with brown sugar. Dissolve 2 tablespoons of instant coffee powder in ⅓ cup hot water and omit cold water.

PEPPERMINT LOW-FAT 7-MINUTE FROSTING: Replace vanilla with ½ teaspoon peppermint extract. After frosting has cooled, fold in ⅓ cup crushed peppermint candies.

Marshmallow Frosting

2 tablespoons milk
6 tablespoons sugar
1 package mini marshmallows
2 tablespoons boiling water
½ teaspoon vanilla extract

1. In a saucepan over low to medium heat warm the milk and sugar for 6 minutes without stirring.

2. In a double boiler heat the marshmallows. When they are very soft, add boiling water, stirring until smooth.

3. Remove from heat. Add the vanilla. With an electric mixer on medium speed beat in the hot sugar. Keep beating until partly cool. Use at once.

Mocha Frosting

¼ pound (1 stick) butter, at
    room temperature
3 cups confectioners' sugar
2 tablespoons coffee grounds,
    coffee liqueur, or strong
    coffee
¼ teaspoon salt
4 large egg yolks
3 tablespoons cocoa
1 tablespoon vanilla extract

1. In a medium bowl cream together the butter and sugar with an electric mixer on medium speed until smooth.

2. Add the remaining ingredients. Beat for 3 minutes. Add more sugar if necessary to reach desired spreading consistency.

Peanut Butter Frosting

12 tablespoons (1½ sticks)
    unsalted butter, at room
    temperature
2 cups firmly packed brown
    sugar
4 tablespoons water
1⅓ cups smooth or crunchy
    peanut butter
2 tablespoons vanilla extract

1. In a saucepan over high heat bring the butter, brown sugar, and water to a boil and continue to boil for 2 minutes. Remove from heat.

2. Stir in the peanut butter and vanilla and beat until smooth. Put the hot frosting on the cupcakes while the cupcakes are still hot. Frosting will thicken as it cools.

Rich Chocolate Frosting

2 tablespoons unsalted butter
¾ cup semisweet chocolate
   chips
6 tablespoons heavy cream
1¼ cups confectioners' sugar
1 teaspoon vanilla extract

1. Place all of the ingredients except for the vanilla in a saucepan. Stir over low heat until smooth. Remove from heat.

2. Stir in the vanilla. Cool slightly. Add more sugar if necessary to achieve desired spreading consistency.

Spread on cupcakes while frosting and cupcakes are still warm.

Root Beer Frosting

1¾ cups confectioners' sugar
¼ cup (½ stick) unsalted
   butter, at room temperature
½ teaspoon vanilla extract
6 tablespoons root beer

1. Gradually add the confectioners' sugar to butter until well mixed.

2. Add the vanilla and root beer. If necessary, add more root beer or confectioners' sugar to reach desired spreading consistency.

Rosewater Icing

½ pound (1½ cups)
   confectioners' sugar
4 teaspoons rosewater
Juice of 1 lemon
2 large egg whites

1. Place all the ingredients in a medium bowl and stir together well.

2. Apply icing to half-cooled cupcakes with a brush. Set in a cool place for 1 hour to dry the icing.

Royal Icing

3 large egg whites
1 pound (3 cups) confectioners'
    sugar
½ teaspoon cream of tartar

1. Place all of the ingredients in a medium bowl and with an electric mixer on low speed beat until blended.

2. Turn mixer to high speed and beat for 7–10 minutes, until icing is the consistency of a stiff meringue. Icing should be thin enough to spread and thick enough to hold its shape.

Spiked Orange Frosting

3 tablespoons orange juice
3 tablespoons orange liqueur
    (Grand Marnier, curaçao,
    or Triple Sec)
3 tablespoons unsalted butter,
    at room temperature
3¾ cups confectioners' sugar
1½ teaspoons orange zest
Few grains salt

1. In a small bowl mix the orange juice and orange liqueur.

2. In a medium bowl cream the butter. Add the sugar to the butter, alternating with orange juice mixture until desired consistency is reached.

3. Stir in zest and salt. Beat with an electric mixer on high speed for 1 minute until creamy.

Strawberry Frosting

6 tablespoons (½ stick)
    unsalted butter, at room
    temperature
One 8-ounce package
    cream cheese, at room
    temperature
4½ cups confectioners' sugar
¾ cup fresh or frozen
    strawberries, sliced
Lemon juice, as needed

1. With an electric mixer on medium speed, cream together the butter, cream cheese, and sugar until smooth.

2. Add the strawberries. Mix well. If you are using fresh strawberries, you might need to add lemon juice to reach a spreadable consistency.

Sugar Paste Icing

1 large egg white
1 tablespoon liquid glucose
3 cups confectioners' sugar, plus
  more for dusting

1. Combine the egg white and glucose in a bowl. Stir with a wooden spoon.

2. Add the confectioners' sugar. Mix with a rubber spatula using a chopping motion until the icing binds together. Knead the mixture with your fingers until it forms a ball.

3. Dust a work surface with confectioners' sugar. Knead the ball until it is soft and pliable.

4. Roll out the icing on the dusted surface until ¼ -inch thick.

5. Cut into shapes with a cookie cutter or knife.

Toasted Coconut Cream Cheese Frosting

4 tablespoons unsalted butter,
  at room temperature
2 cups flaked coconut
One 8-ounce package cream
  cheese, at room
  temperature
2 cups confectioners' sugar
2 teaspoons milk
1 teaspoon vanilla extract

1. Melt 2 tablespoons of the butter in a large skillet over medium heat. Stir in the coconut and cook, stirring constantly, until coconut is golden brown, about 8 minutes.

2. In a bowl cream the remaining butter and the cream cheese with an electric mixer on medium speed until smooth and creamy. Add the confectioners' sugar, milk, and vanilla slowly, beating after each addition. Beat until smooth. Stir in the toasted coconut.

Vanilla Frosting

3 cups confectioners' sugar
½ cup (1 stick) unsalted butter,
  at room temperature
2 teaspoons vanilla extract
2 tablespoons milk

1. Gradually add the sugar to the softened butter and cream together with an electric mixer.

2. Stir in the vanilla and milk. Beat until smooth and of spreading consistency. Add a litle more milk or sugar as needed.

LICORICE FROSTING: Substitute 2 teaspoons licorice or anise extract for vanilla.

Vegan Chocolate Icing

1 cup vegan granulated sugar
6 tablespoons cornstarch
4 tablespoons cocoa powder
½ teaspoon salt
1 cup water
2 tablespoons vegetable oil
½ teaspoon vanilla extract

1. Mix the sugar, cornstarch, cocoa, and salt in a medium saucepan. Whisk in the water and cook over medium heat, stirring constantly, until it thickens and starts to boil. Boil for 1–2 minutes. Don't overcook. Remove from the heat.

2. Stir in oil and vanilla. Cool before using.

Vegan Cream Cheese Frosting

½ cup soy margarine, at room temperature
3 ounces tofu cream cheese, at room temperature
2 tablespoons soy or rice milk
4 cups vegan confectioners' sugar
1 tablespoon lemon juice
1 teaspoon vanilla extract

1. In a large bowl cream together the margarine, cream cheese, and milk with an electric mixer on medium speed.

2. Add the sugar slowly, beating constantly, until combined.

3. Add the lemon juice and vanilla and beat until light and fluffy. If necessary, add more sugar or milk to reach desired consistency.

VEGAN BERRY ICING: Add ¼ cup mashed fresh or frozen berries.

VEGAN COFFEE ICING: Substitute espresso for the soy or rice milk. Add 1 tablespoon ground espresso beans.

Whipped Cream

1½ cups whipping cream
1 teaspoon vanilla extract
2 tablespoons granulated sugar

1. In a medium bowl whip the cream, vanilla, and sugar with an electric mixer on high speed until thick.

CINNAMON WHIPPED CREAM: Add ½ teaspoon ground cinnamon before whipping.

White Chocolate Buttercream Frosting

1½ cups (9 ounces) white
    chocolate chips
4 tablespoons (½ stick)
    unsalted butter, at room
    temperature
3 tablespoons milk
1 teaspoon vanilla extract
4½ cups confectioners' sugar

1. Heat the white chocolate chips, butter, and milk in a saucepan over medium heat until all is melted. Remove from heat.

2. Stir in the vanilla. Add the confectioners' sugar slowly, stirring constantly, until combined. Add more milk or sugar to achieve desired spreading consistency.

White Chocolate Mint Frosting

½ cup whipping cream
1 tablespoon unsalted butter
8 ounces white chocolate,
    chopped
1 tablespoon green crème de
    menthe

1. Bring the cream and butter to a simmer in a small saucepan over medium heat. Stir until the butter melts. Remove from heat.

2. Add the white chocolate. Stir until melted.

3. Mix in the crème de menthe. Cool at room temperature for 2 hours.

TOPPING RECIPES

Candied Citrus Peel

1 cup granulated sugar
½ cup water
2 tablespoons corn syrup
Rind of 2 oranges, washed, cut
    into very thin strips
Rind of 2 lemons, washed, cut
    into very thin strips
Rind of 2 limes, washed, cut
    into very thin strips

1. In a saucepan over medium-high heat bring the sugar, water, and corn syrup to a boil. Add the rinds and boil for 20 minutes, stirring occasionally.

2. Remove from heat and, using tongs, place the peels on a wire cooling rack. Dry the peels overnight. Use as an edible garnish or add to recipes.

Caramel Topping

½ cup packed light brown sugar
4 tablespoons (½ stick) unsalted butter
¼ cup heavy cream
1 teaspoon vanilla extract

1. In a saucepan over medium heat bring the brown sugar, butter, and cream to a boil. Reduce heat to a simmer and continue stirring for 5 minutes. Remove from heat.
2. Stir in the vanilla.
3. Pour the warm caramel topping over cupcakes.

Celebration Cookies

½ pound (2 sticks) unsalted butter, softened
1 cup granulated sugar
1 large egg
1 teaspoon vanilla extract
3 cups all-purpose flour
2 teaspoons baking powder

1. Preheat the oven to 400°F.
2. In a large bowl cream together the butter and sugar with an electric mixer on medium speed until fluffy. Add the egg and vanilla and mix well.
3. In a separate bowl combine the flour and baking powder.
4. Slowly add the dry ingredients to the butter mixture, stirring with a wooden spoon until all of the flour is incorporated.
5. On a lightly floured surface roll out half of the dough to ⅛-inch thickness. Dip cookie cutters into flour and cut shapes out of the dough. Place cookies on an ungreased baking sheet. Repeat with the remaining dough.
6. Bake until cookies are golden around the edges, about 4–6 minutes.
7. Cool cookies slightly in the pan before removing them. Top with your favorite frosting.

Yields about 48 cookies, depending on the size of your cookie cutters.

• To vary the flavor of your cookies, add 2 tablespoons of citrus zest or 1 teaspoon of your favorite flavored extract.

Chocolate Chip Cookies

2 1/4 cups flour
1 teaspoon baking soda
1 teaspoon salt
1 cup unsalted butter, at
    room temperature
3/4 cup granulated sugar
3/4 cup firmly packed brown
    sugar
1 teaspoon vanilla extract
1/2 cup water
2 large eggs
2 cups (12 ounces) semisweet
    chocolate chips
1 cup chopped nuts

1. Preheat the oven to 375°F. Lightly grease baking sheets.

2. In a medium bowl combine the flour, baking soda, and salt. Set aside.

3. In a separate bowl beat together the butter, sugars, vanilla, and water until creamy. Add the eggs and beat until smooth.

4. Slowly add the dry ingredients to the wet ingredients, mixing until all the flour has been incorporated.

5. Stir in the chocolate chips and nuts.

6. Drop dough by 1/2 teaspoon measurements onto the baking pan.

7. Bake 10–12 minutes or until golden. Cool and remove from the baking pan with a spatula.

Yields about 48 cookies.

Crystal Edible Flowers

2 large egg whites
Edible flowers (see page 97 for
    examples)
1 cup superfine sugar

1. Place the egg whites in a small bowl. Using a small brush lightly coat the top and underside of each flower.

2. Sprinkle sugar on the top and underside of each flower.

3. Place flowers on waxed paper or parchment paper. Set until firm, about 1 hour.

Edible Flowers

DANDELION	Young flowers are the sweetest. They taste like honey.
CHAMOMILE	These small daisylike flowers have a sweet, apple flavor.
CHRYSANTHEMUM	Tangy; wide range of colors including red, white, yellow, and orange.
LAVENDER	Sweet, floral flavor.
MINT	Leaves and flowers can be eaten. The flavor of the flowers is bright and familiar.
PRIMROSE	Colorful and sweet.
PANSY	Pansy petals have a mild grassy flavor.
ROSE	Light-colored roses have a mild flavor; darker varieties are stronger. Miniature varieties or loose petals can be crystallized.
SCENTED GERANIUM	A lemon-scented geranium will have lemon-flavored flowers. A mint-scented geranium will have mint-flavored flowers.
VIOLET	Sweet, perfumed flavor.

NOTE: Some people have allergies to flowers just like any other food. These flowers are edible for most individuals.

Dark Chocolate Sauce

1 cup half-and-half
½ cup granulated sugar
¼ cup dark chocolate, coarsely chopped
3 tablespoons butter
1 teaspoon vanilla extract

1. In a saucepan over low heat whisk the half-and-half, sugar, chocolate, and butter until sugar dissolves and butter melts. Increase to medium heat and whisk until sauce begins to simmer. Remove from heat.

2. Stir in the vanilla. Cool before serving.

Gingerbread Men Cookies

6 tablespoons (¾ stick) unsalted butter, at room temperature
¾ cup firmly packed brown sugar
1 large egg
½ cup molasses
2 teaspoons vanilla extract
1 teaspoon grated lemon zest
3 cups all-purpose flour
1½ teaspoons baking powder
¾ teaspoon baking soda
¼ teaspoon salt
1 tablespoon ground ginger
1¾ teaspoons ground cinnamon
¼ teaspoon ground cloves
Red cinnamon imperials

1. Preheat the oven to 375°F. Grease baking sheets.

2. In a large bowl beat together the butter, brown sugar, and egg until smooth. Add the molasses, vanilla, and zest. Beat until well combined.

3. In a separate bowl combine the flour, baking powder, baking soda, salt, ginger, cinnamon, and cloves.

4. Slowly add the dry ingredients to the wet ingredients and mix until well blended.

5. Divide the dough into two balls and place them back into the bowls. Cover the bowls with plastic wrap and let them sit at room temperature for 2 hours.

6. On a lightly floured surface roll out the dough to a ¼-inch thickness. Cut the cookies with a small gingerbread man cutter. Carefully place cookies on cookie sheets.

7. Place red cinnamon imperials on the cookies to look like eyes and buttons.

8. Bake until edges of cookies are lightly browned, 6–10 minutes.

9. Frost and decorate as you like.

Yields about 48 cookies, depending on the size of your cookie cutters.

Hot Fudge

⅔ cup (4 ounces) unsweetened
    chocolate, coarsely chopped
¼ pound (1 stick) unsalted
    butter
½ teaspoon salt
3 cups granulated sugar
One 12-ounce can evaporated
    milk

1. In a double boiler melt the chocolate, butter, and salt together.

2. Add the sugar, ½ cup at a time, stirring after each addition until melted. Slowly add the evaporated milk until fully integrated.

Marzipan

2¼ cups finely ground
    almonds
1 cup confectioners' sugar, plus
    more for dusting
1 cup superfine sugar
1 teaspoon lemon juice
½ teaspoon almond extract
1 large egg

1. Combine the almonds, confectioners' sugar, and superfine sugar in a bowl and mix well. Add the lemon juice, almond extract, and egg. Mix well and then gather together with your fingers to form a ball.

2. On a surface lightly dusted with confectioners' sugar knead the marzipan until smooth.

Mocha Sauce

1⅓ cups (8 ounces) dark
    chocolate, coarsely chopped
1 cup heavy cream
½ cup strong brewed coffee
1 teaspoon vanilla extract

1. Place the chocolate in a bowl.

2. In a small saucepan bring the heavy cream and coffee to a boil over medium-high heat.

3. Pour the mixture over the chocolate. Gently whisk until the chocolate is completely melted and the sauce is smooth. Stir in the vanilla.

Orange Sauce

2 tablespoons granulated sugar
2 tablespoons orange zest
1 cup orange juice
½ cup orange marmalade

1. In a small saucepan over medium heat stir together all the ingredients until sugar and marmalade are melted. Cool.

Raspberry Sauce

2 cups fresh or frozen
   raspberries
3 tablespoons granulated sugar
½ teaspoon lemon juice

1. In a blender or food processor puree the raspberries, sugar, and lemon juice until smooth. If you would like a smoother sauce, pour through a fine sieve into a bowl.

2. Heat the sauce in a saucepan over medium heat until sugar is melted. Serve the sauce hot or cold.

Rice Cereal Topping

2 tablespoons (¼ stick)
   unsalted butter
1½ cup marshmallows
2 cups puffed rice cereal

1. Melt the butter in a saucepan over low heat. Add the marshmallows and stir until completely melted. Remove from heat.

2. Add the rice cereal. Stir until rice cereal is well coated.

Rum Syrup

1 cup granulated sugar
½ cup water
1 teaspoon (1 pat) unsalted
   butter
1 teaspoon vanilla extract
3 tablespoons rum

1. In a saucepan over medium-high heat bring the sugar and water to a boil. Boil for 5 minutes. Add the butter, vanilla, and rum. Cook until the mixture becomes thick and syrupy. While syrup is still hot, top the cupcakes.

Strawberry Sauce

2 cups fresh or frozen
   strawberries
5 tablespoons granulated sugar
1 teaspoon lemon juice

1. In a blender or food processor puree the strawberries, sugar, and lemon juice until smooth.

2. Heat the sauce in a saucepan over medium heat until sugar is melted. Serve the sauce hot or cold.

Streusel Topping

⅓ cup firmly packed brown
   sugar
¼ cup granulated sugar
1 teaspoon ground cinnamon
1 cup chopped walnuts

1. Combine all ingredients in a bowl. Blend well.

Walnut Apple Raisin Topping

3 tablespoons unsalted butter
1½ cups chopped apples
1 cup chopped walnuts
½ teaspoon ground cinnamon
½ cup golden raisins
3 tablespoons lemon juice
3 tablespoons brown sugar

1. In a skillet melt the butter over medium heat. Add the apples, walnuts, and cinnamon and sauté for 3–5 minutes or until apples are lightly browned. Remove from heat and transfer to a bowl.

2. Add the raisins, lemon juice, and brown sugar. Mix well.

White Chocolate Sauce

⅔ cup (4 ounces) white
   chocolate, chopped
¾ cup heavy cream

1. Melt the white chocolate in a saucepan over low heat or in the microwave.

2. In a separate saucepan, heat the cream over high heat to boiling.

3. Whisk the cream into the melted chocolate until smooth. Refrigerate until ready to use.

Irish Cream Filling

One 3.4-ounce package instant
    vanilla pudding
¾ cup milk
¾ cup heavy whipping cream
3 tablespoons Irish cream
    liqueur

1. Place all of the ingredients in a mixing bowl and beat with an electric mixer on low speed until blended and smooth.

2. Increase to high speed and continue beating until the filling is light and fluffy. Do not overbeat.

Pastry Cream

½ cup granulated sugar
¼ cup cornstarch
4 large egg yolks
2 cups milk
½ teaspoon vanilla extract

1. In a medium bowl mix together ¼ cup of the sugar and the cornstarch. Add the egg yolks and mix until a paste is formed. Stir in ½ cup of the milk.

2. In a saucepan over medium-high heat bring the remaining 1½ cups milk and the remaining ¼ cup sugar to a boil.

3. Pour hot mixture into the egg mixture. Beat well.

4. Pour the mixture back into the saucepan and cook over medium heat until thick and smooth. Remove from heat.

5. Stir in the vanilla and mix for an additional minute. Cover and chill for 2 hours.

Tiramisù Cream

3 large eggs, separated
4 tablespoons granulated sugar
One 8-ounce container
   mascarpone cheese or
   cream cheese
2 tablespoons Kahlúa or
   amaretto

1. With an electric mixer on medium-high speed beat the egg yolks with sugar until fluffy. Add the cheese and beat until smooth. Stir in the liqueur.

2. In a separate bowl with clean beaters mix the egg whites until shiny and stiff peaks form.

3. Fold the egg whites into the cheese mixture until well blended.

Clockwise from top: Oatmeal Banana Cupcake, Coffee Cupcake, Lemon Poppy Seed Cupcake, Sour Cream Coffee Cake Cupcake, Blueberry Cupcake.

chapter 4

Everyday Cupcakes

BREAKFAST CUPCAKES

Everyone knows the best way to start the day is with a good breakfast. Muffins are a classic first-thing-in-the-morning food, but cupcakes are eye opening and energizing. What's the difference between the two? Muffins are dense while cupcakes are light and cakelike. Muffins are usually not frosted—cupcakes are (yum). Bake cupcakes the night before and eat them on the go in the morning or savor them at a leisurely weekend brunch.

BLUEBERRY CUPCAKES

You will need:

Blueberry Cupcakes recipe (page 52)
Maple Cream Cheese Frosting recipe (page 86)
Honey
Fresh blueberries

1. Drizzle honey on the frosted cupcakes to make a pattern.
2. Garnish with fresh blueberries.

COFFEE CUPCAKES

You will need:

Coffee Cupcakes recipe (page 60)
Coffee Cream Cheese Frosting recipe (page 85)
Chocolate-covered espresso beans

1. Top frosted cupcakes with chocolate-covered espresso beans.

LEMON POPPY SEED CUPCAKES

You will need:

Lemon Ginger Poppy Seed Cupcakes recipe (page 66)
Lemon Icing recipe (page 87)
White Chocolate Buttercream Frosting recipe (page 94)
Poppy seeds

Pastry bag with petal tip

1. Place the buttercream icing in a pastry bag and make a flower shape on lemon-iced cupcakes.
2. Sprinkle poppy seeds in the center of the flower.

OATMEAL BANANA CUPCAKES

You will need:

Oatmeal Raisin Cupcakes recipe (page 70)
Banana Coconut Frosting recipe (page 83)
Granola
Banana chips
Raisins

1. Pour the granola into a small bowl. Dip the freshly frosted cupcakes into the granola.
2. Top with banana chips and raisins.

SOUR CREAM COFFEE CAKE CUPCAKES

You will need:

Sour Cream Coffee Cake Cupcakes recipe (page 77)
Streusel Topping recipe (page 101)
Lemon Icing recipe (page 87)

1. Bake, frost, and add topping to the cupcakes.
2. Drizzle icing over the tops of the cupcakes.

HIDDEN SURPRISES CUPCAKES

These treat-filled cupcakes hark back to those many of us relished as kids. Discovering the secret cream, jam, fruit, candy, or pudding filling is still a thrilling surprise. And mixing cupcake batters in layers or swirled patterns is a terrific way to keep your taste buds guessing. Try the other flavor combinations in Chapter 9.

CANDY-FILLED CUPCAKES

You will need:

Golden Cupcakes (page 64) or Chocolate Cupcakes recipe (page 58)
Chocolate Ganache recipe (page 84)
Chocolate Frosting recipe (page 84)
Chocolate candies

Pastry bag with writing tip

1. Remove two teaspoons of cake in cone shapes from the centers of the cupcakes with a grapefruit spoon. Save the removed cake. Fill each hole with a chocolate candy. Replace the cake and trim the tops of the cupcakes so that they are even.
2. Dip the cupcakes in ganache. Chill for 1 hour to firm.
3. Fill a pastry bag with frosting and decorate the cupcakes with line patterns.

CREAM-FILLED CUPCAKES

You will need:

Cream-Filled Cupcakes recipe (page 62)
Pastry Cream recipe (page 102)
Chocolate Ganache recipe (page 84)
Vanilla Frosting recipe (page 92)

Pastry bag with writing tip

1. Remove two teaspoons of cake in cone shapes from the centers of the cupcakes with a grapefruit spoon. Save the removed cake. Fill the holes with Pastry Cream. Replace the cake and trim the tops of the cupcakes so that they are even.

2. Dip the cupcakes in ganache. Chill for 1 hour to firm.

3. Fill a pastry bag with frosting and decorate the cupcakes with line patterns.

LAYERED CHOCOLATE MINT CUPCAKES

You will need:

Chocolate Cupcakes recipe (page 58)
Peppermint Cupcakes recipe (page 73)
Chocolate Frosting recipe (page 84)
Peppermint Cream Cheese Frosting recipe (page 86)
Chocolate candies
Peppermint candies

1. Prepare the cupcake batters. Fill the cupcake liners one-third full with the chocolate batter. Pour the Peppermint Cupcakes batter over the chocolate batter until the cups are two-thirds full. Bake and cool.

2. Frost half the cupcakes with Chocolate Frosting and the other half with Peppermint Cream Cheese Frosting. Swirl the frostings together with a knife.

3. Top with chocolate and peppermint candies.

Clockwise from top: Cream-Filled Cupcake, Swirled Vanilla, Chocolate, and Strawberry Cupcake, Candy-Filled Cupcake, Layered Chocolate Mint Cupcake, Swirled Peanut Butter Chocolate Cupcake.

Cupcake Bar

Frazzled over what to take to potluck gatherings? Want to keep the guests awake at a slumber party? Create a Cupcake Bar that'll be the talk of the party.

Beforehand, prepare your favorite cupcakes and frosting. You can either frost the cupcakes or have guests frost their own. Surround the cupcakes with bowls of toppings, include shredded coconut, chopped nuts, toffee bits, crushed cookies, sprinkles, and candies. Invite guests to create their own custom cupcakes. Some cupcakes will be topped simply and daintily, others will simply be over the top. All varieties will be delicious!

SWIRLED PEANUT BUTTER CHOCOLATE CUPCAKES

You will need:
  Peanut Butter Cupcakes recipe (page 71)
  Chocolate Cupcakes recipe (page 58)
  Peanut Butter Frosting recipe (page 89)
  Chocolate Frosting recipe (page 84)
  Peanuts
  Chocolate

1. Prepare the cupcake batters. In a large bowl lightly swirl the two batters together. Fill cupcake liners three-quarters full. Bake and cool.

2. Prepare the frostings. Apply Peanut Butter Frosting to half of each cupcake. Apply Chocolate Frosting to the other half. With a knife swirl the frostings together.

3. Top with peanuts and chocolate.

SWIRLED VANILLA, CHOCOLATE, AND STRAWBERRY CUPCAKES

You will need:
  Golden Cupcakes recipe (page 64)
  Chocolate Cupcakes recipe (page 58)
  Strawberry Cupcakes recipe (page 78)
  Vanilla Frosting recipe (page 92)
  Chocolate Frosting recipe (page 84)
  Strawberry Frosting recipe (page 91)
  White chocolate
  Chocolate
  Fresh strawberries

1. Fill the cupcake liners one-quarter full with the Golden Cupcakes batter. Top with Chocolate Cupcakes batter until liners are half full. Top with Strawberry Cupcakes batter until cupcake liners are three-quarters full. Bake and cool.

2. Frost cupcakes in a bull's-eye pattern with Vanilla, Chocolate, and Strawberry Frostings.

3. Top cupcakes with white chocolate, chocolate, and strawberries.

HEALTHY CUPCAKES

I believe the approaches to making delicious and healthy cupcakes are infinite. These recipes are low in fat and high in luxury. They are sweet, light, and rich. There are some suggestions for vegan cupcakes, too.

LOW-FAT CARROT CUPCAKES

You will need:

    Low-Fat Carrot Cupcakes recipe (page 67)
    Low-Fat Cream Cheese Frosting recipe (page 88)
    Whole nuts
    Dried fruits
    Raisins

1. Decorate frosted cupcakes with whole nuts, dried fruits, and raisins to create a flower.

LOW-FAT CHOCOLATE CUPCAKES

You will need:

    Low-Fat Chocolate Cupcakes recipe (page 67)
    Low-Fat Chocolate Frosting recipe (page 88)
    Chocolate pieces, chopped
    Chocolate candies

1. Pour the chocolate pieces into a small bowl. Dip the freshly frosted cupcakes into the chocolate.
2. Top with a whole chocolate candy.

LOW-FAT WHITE CUPCAKES

You will need:

 Low-Fat White Cupcakes recipe (page 68)
 Low-Fat 7-Minute Frosting recipe (page 88)
 Assorted fresh berries

1. Top frosted cupcakes with assorted fresh berries.

VEGAN CHOCOLATE CUPCAKES

You will need:
Vegan Chocolate Cupcakes recipe (page 79)
Vegan Chocolate Icing recipe (page 93)
Nuts, chopped and whole

1. Pour the chopped nuts into a small bowl. Dip the freshly iced cupcakes into the nuts.
2. Place a whole nut in the center of each top to create a flower.

VEGAN WHITE CUPCAKES

You will need:
Vegan White Cupcakes recipe (page 80)
Vegan Cream Cheese Frosting recipe (page 93)
Flaked coconut
Fresh berries

1. Pour the coconut into a small bowl. Dip the edges of the freshly iced cupcakes into the coconut.
2. Top with fresh berries.

On plate, clockwise from top: Low-Fat Carrot Cupcake, Vegan Chocolate Cupcake, Vegan White Cupcake. On napkin, left to right: Low-Fat Chocolate Cupcake, Low-Fat White Cupcake. Bottom: Zucchini Cupcake

ZUCCHINI CUPCAKES

You will need:
Zucchini Cupcakes recipe (page 81)
Low-Fat Cream Cheese Frosting (page 88) or Low-Fat Chocolate Frosting recipe (page 88)
Sunflower seeds
Whole nuts

1. Top frosted cupcakes with sunflower seeds and whole nuts to create flower patterns.

COOKIE AND CANDY CUPCAKES

Everybody has a cookie or candy they'd wrestle a bull for. Whether you'd tempt fate for the taste of a classic chocolate chip or oatmeal raisin cookie, this nostalgic candy bar collection of recipes, based on time-tested cookie and candy flavors, is a sure (and much safer) bet.

COOKIES AND CREAM CUPCAKES

You will need:

Cookies and Cream Cupcakes recipe (page 61)
Vanilla Frosting recipe (page 92)
Chocolate sandwich cookies, crumbled and whole

1. Place cookie crumbs in a small bowl. Add crushed cookies around the edges of each cupcake.
2. Top with a whole chocolate sandwich cookie.

GINGERSNAP CUPCAKES

You will need:

Gingerbread Cupcakes recipe (page 64)
Ginger Cream Cheese Frosting recipe (page 86)
Gingersnaps, crushed and whole

1. Place the cookie crumbs in a small bowl. Add crushed cookies around the edges of each cupcake.
2. Top with a whole gingersnap cookie.

HOMEMADE CHOCOLATE CHIP COOKIE CUPCAKES

You will need:

Piping gel
Chocolate Chip Cookie Cupcakes recipe (page 57)
Chocolate Chip Cookies recipe (page 96)

1. Attach a chocolate chip cookie to frosted cupcake tops.

Front row: Cookies and Cream Cupcake. Middle row, left to right: Mix-In Chewy Candy Cupcake, Oatmeal Raisin Cupcake, Mix-In Chocolate Fruit Cupcake. Top row, left to right: Mix-In Candy Bar Cupcake, Homemade Chocolate Chip Cookie Cupcake, Gingersnap Cupcake.

MIX-IN CANDY BAR CUPCAKES

You will need:

Golden Cupcakes (page 64) or Chocolate Cupcakes recipe (page 58)
Chocolate Frosting recipe (page 84)
Assorted regular-sized candy bars, chopped
Assorted mini candy bars

1. Fill the cupcake liners two-thirds full with cupcake batter.

2. Chop an assortment of your favorite candy bars into small pieces and place in separate bowls. Spoon different candy pieces into the batter-filled liners. Bake and cool.

3. Divide the frosting into several small bowls. Add pieces of assorted candy bars to each bowl of frosting. Stir, then frost the cupcakes.

4. Top with whole mini candy bars.

MIX-IN CHEWY CANDY CUPCAKES

You will need:

Golden Cupcakes (page 64) or Chocolate Cupcakes recipe (page 58)
Chocolate Frosting (page 84) or Vanilla Frosting recipe (page 92)
Assorted chewy candies

1. Fill the cupcake liners two-thirds full with cupcakes batter.

2. Push assorted chewy candies into the batter. Bake and cool.

3. Divide the frosting into several small bowls. Chop chewy candies and add them to each bowl of frosting. Frost the cupcakes.

4. Top with chewy candies.

MIX-IN CHOCOLATE FRUIT CUPCAKES

You will need:

Chocolate Cupcakes recipe (page 58)
Chocolate Frosting recipe (page 84)
Assorted fresh berries and fruits

1. Fill cupcake liners two-thirds full with batter.

2. Place different berry and fruit combinations into the batter-filled cups. Bake and cool.

3. Divide the frosting into several small bowls. Add different berries and fruits to the frosting. Crush them while stirring. Frost the cupcakes.

4. Garnish with fresh fruits and berries.

OATMEAL RAISIN CUPCAKES

You will need:

Oatmeal Raisin Cupcakes recipe (page 70)
Maple Cream Cheese Frosting recipe (page 86)
Chewy oatmeal cookies
Chocolate-covered raisins

1. Place a chewy oatmeal cookie on each frosted cupcake top.
2. Decorate with chocolate-covered raisins.

TOTALLY CHOCOLATE CUPCAKES

When it comes to chocolate, sometimes one small ultra-rich bite satisfies our craving. Other times we want to indulge in more than one. The following pop-in-your-mouth mini cupcakes are packed with flavor, and their size is an irresistible invitation to eat as many as you like. If you want to splurge, the extra large cupcakes are huge and sensational.

EXTRA LARGE BITTERSWEET MOLTEN CHOCOLATE CUPCAKES

You will need:

Bittersweet Molten Chocolate Cupcakes recipe (page 51)
Whipped Cream recipe (page 93)

Large cupcake pan

1. Top warm cupcakes with Whipped Cream. Serve warm.

Clockwise, from top: Extra Large German Chocolate Cupcake, Extra Large Bittersweet Molten Chocolate Cupcake, Mini Chocolate Mousse Cupcake, Extra Large White Chocolate Cupcake, Mini Rich Chocolate Cupcale.

EXTRA LARGE GERMAN CHOCOLATE CUPCAKES

You will need:

German Chocolate Cupcakes recipe (page 63)
Coconut Pecan Frosting recipe (page 85)
Chocolate Frosting recipe (page 84)
Pecans
Chocolate

Large cupcake pan

1. Frost the cupcake tops with Coconut Pecan Frosting in the center and with Chocolate Frosting around the perimeter.

2. Top with pecans and chocolate.

EXTRA LARGE WHITE CHOCOLATE CUPCAKES

You will need:

White Chocolate Cupcakes recipe (page 80)
White Chocolate Buttercream recipe (page 94)
White chocolate chunks

Large cupcake pan

1. Top frosted large cupcakes with white chocolate chunks.

MINI CHOCOLATE MOUSSE CUPCAKES

You will need:

Mousse Cupcakes recipe (page 70)
Whipped Cream recipe (page 93)
Cocoa powder
Chocolate pieces

Mini cupcake pans

1. Spoon Whipped Cream onto baked and cooled mini cupcakes.
2. Sprinkle on cocoa and top with chocolate pieces.

MINI RICH CHOCOLATE CUPCAKES

You will need:

Rich Chocolate Cupcakes recipe (page 75)
Rich Chocolate Frosting recipe (page 90)
Chocolate Curls (see page 39)

Mini cupcake pans

1. Top frosted mini cupcakes with Chocolate Curls.

Front row, left to right: Caramel Nut Sundae Cupcake, Banana Split Cupcake. Back row, left to right: Root Beer Float Cupcake, Hot Fudge Sundae Cupcake, Creamsicle Cupcake

ICE CREAM CUPCAKES

Ice cream is always a refreshing treat, even in the middle of winter. Here is a selection of frozen fantasies that transform ice cream and cupcakes into rich, creamy sundaes. They are sure to bring back memories of hanging out with friends at the ice cream parlor.

BANANA SPLIT CUPCAKES

You will need:
> *Banana Cupcakes recipe (page 50)*
> *Vanilla or chocolate ice cream*
> *Sliced bananas or banana chips*
> *Whipped Cream recipe (page 93)*
> *Chocolate syrup*
> *Maraschino cherries*

1. Scoop ice cream onto the baked cupcakes. Place sliced bananas or banana chips on top. Spoon on Whipped Cream. Pour on chocolate syrup and top with a maraschino cherry.

CARAMEL NUT SUNDAE CUPCAKES

You will need:
> *Vanilla ice cream*
> *Maple Walnut Cupcakes recipe (page 68)*
> *Caramel Topping recipe (page 95)*
> *Walnuts*
> *Caramel candies*

1. Scoop vanilla ice cream onto baked cupcakes. Pour Caramel Topping over the ice cream. Sprinkle on nuts.
2. Garnish with caramel candies.

CREAMSICLE CUPCAKES

You will need:
> *Orange Cupcakes recipe (page 76)*
> *Vanilla ice cream*
> *Orange sorbet*
> *Orange Sauce recipe (page 100)*
> *Whipped Cream recipe (page 93)*
> *Orange colored sugar*
> *Orange candy*

1. Scoop the vanilla ice cream and orange sorbet onto baked cupcakes. Pour on the Orange Sauce. Top with Whipped Cream.

2. Sprinkle on orange sugar and candy.

HOT FUDGE SUNDAE CUPCAKES

You will need:
Sugar cones
Vanilla or chocolate ice cream
Bittersweet Molten Chocolate Cupcakes recipe (page 51)
Hot Fudge recipe (page 99)
Whipped Cream recipe (page 93)
Nuts (walnuts or peanuts)
Maraschino cherries

1. Break each sugar cone about 2½ inches above the point. Reserve the points. Crush the remaining part of the cones into pieces.

2. Scoop ice cream onto the baked cupcakes. Pour Hot Fudge over the ice cream. Top with Whipped Cream.

3. Stick the sugar cone point into the Whipped Cream. Sprinkle on nuts, a maraschino cherry, and remaining sugar cone pieces.

ROOT BEER FLOAT CUPCAKES

You will need:
Vanilla ice cream
Root Beer Cupcakes recipe (page 63)
Root Beer Frosting recipe (page 90)
Root beer candies, whole and crushed

1. Scoop the ice cream onto the frosted cupcakes.

2. Top with whole and crushed root beer candies.

chapter 5

Parties

TEA PARTY PETIT FOUR CUPCAKES

Petit four cupcakes combine two European traditions—British high tea and French pastry making. Host an afternoon tea, which is quintessentially British, and serve petit four cupcakes, which are small French cakes that are traditionally served after dessert. Tiny delights made from single and double layer mini cupcakes provide an elegant treat for a playful tea party.

When these party refreshments are double layered, you will bake two mini cupcakes for each completed cupcake. The bottom layers remain in their cupcake liners, while the upper layers can be baked directly in a greased tin without a liner or baked and then removed from the liner. Note: The baking time will be 5–7 minutes shorter than for medium-sized cupcakes.

FOR EACH RECIPE:

1. Bake the cupcakes in mini cupcake pans. Let them cool.

2. Divide the cupcakes in half. Half the batch will be used as the top layers and the other half will be the bottom layers. If the cupcakes are baked in liners, remove the top layers from their liners.

3. Apply jam or frosting to the tops of the bottom-layer cupcakes.

4. Turn the top-layer cupcakes upside down and place them on the bottom layers. Frost the top-layer cupcakes.

5. Dip the petit four cupcakes into nuts, coconut, and toppings.

CHOCOLATE PIPING PETIT FOUR CUPCAKES

You will need:
   Chocolate Cupcakes recipe (page 58)
   Vanilla Frosting recipe (page 92)
   Food coloring
   Fruit jam
   Chocolate

   Mini cupcake pans
   Pastry bag with small writing tip

1. Divide the frosting into several bowls, add food coloring to each, and stir.

2. Spread jam on the tops of the bottom-layer cupcakes.

3. Remove the liners and flip the top-layer cupcakes upside down and place on top of the bottom-layer cakes. Frost the top-layer cupcakes on all sides.

4. Melt the chocolate and decorate the cupcake tops with piped chocolate designs.

LEMON BERRY COCONUT PETIT FOUR CUPCAKES

These cupcakes can be made with blueberries, blackberries, raspberries, strawberries, or any other type of small berry. Match the berry jam fillings with the berry toppings or be creative and mix the flavors.

You will need:
Lemon Cupcakes recipe (page 66)
Toasted Coconut Cream Cheese Frosting recipe (page 92)
Berry jam
Shredded coconut
Fresh berries or frosted berries (see page 46)
Lemon zest knot (see page 47)

Mini cupcake pans

1. Spread jam on the tops of the bottom-layer cupcakes.
2. Remove the liners, flip the top-layer cupcakes upside down and place on top of the bottom-layer cakes. Frost the top-layer cupcakes on all sides.
3. Pour some shredded coconut into a small bowl. Dip the freshly iced cupcakes into the coconut.
4. Dip the berry bottoms and the lemon zest into the icing. Place on the cupcake tops.

LICORICE PETIT FOUR CUPCAKES

You will need:
Licorice Cupcakes recipe (page 64)
Licorice Frosting recipe (page 92)
Food coloring
Fruit jam
Licorice candies

Mini cupcake pans

1. Divide the frosting into several bowls, add food coloring to each, and stir.
2. Spread jam on the tops of the bottom-layer cupcakes.
3. Remove the liners, flip the top-layer cupcakes upside down and place on top of the bottom-layer cakes. Frost the top-layer cupcakes on all sides.
4. Decorate with licorice candies.

MARZIPAN PETIT FOUR CUPCAKES

You will need:
Almond Cupcakes recipe (page 49)
Marzipan fruits (see pages 42–44)
Almond Frosting recipe (page 83)
Food coloring
Toasted chopped almonds

Mini cupcake pans

1. Shape marzipan into fruits of your choice.

2. Divide the frosting into several bowls, add food coloring to each and stir. Reserve a few tablespoons of frosting to use as glue. Spread frosting on the tops of the bottom-layer cupcakes.

3. Remove the liners, flip the top-layer cupcakes upside down and placae on top of the bottom-layer cakes. Frost the top-layer cupcakes on all sides

4. Pour the almonds into a small bowl. Dip the cupcakes into the almonds.

5. Use the frosting to glue the marzipan fruits to the tops of cupcakes.

MINT CHOCOLATE CHIP PETIT FOUR CUPCAKES

You will need:
Mint Chocolate Chip Cupcakes recipe (page 69)
White Chocolate Mint Frosting recipe (page 94)
Mint chips
Chocolate pieces
Mint leaves

Mini cupcake pans

1. Spread frosting on the tops of the bottom-layer cupcakes. Press mint chips into the bottom-layer cupcakes until flat.

2. Remove the liners, flip the top-layer cupcakes upside down and

On cake plate: clockwise from far left: Chocolate Covered Fruit Petit Four Cupcake, Lemon Berry Coconut Cupcake, Mint Chocolate Chip Petit Four Cupcake, Sesame Chocolate-Covered Strawberries Petit Four Cupcake, Marzipan Petit Four Cupcake, Licorice Petit Four Cupcake, Mint Chocolate Chip Petit Four Cupcake. Center: Lemon Berry Cocout Petit Four Cupcake. On napkin, Marzipan Petit Four Cupcake. On tabletop: Chocolate Piping Petit Four Cupcake.

Create Cupcakes

*A*re you looking for a new way to get people talking at your party? Hand-decorating cupcakes makes an entertaining icebreaker. Before your party, prepare Blank Canvas Cupcakes (opposite) and set the table with decorating tools like edible markers, food coloring, brushes, and watercolor palettes. (As you'll discover, applying food coloring to smooth sugar paste icing is a lot like painting a watercolor). Fill a pastry bag with frosting so that your guests can add frames to their artwork.

When your guests have gathered around the table, encourage them to paint their "canvasses" with flowers and landscapes, whimsical patterns and abstract designs. To initiate further mingling, find a place to display their creations and precede dessert with a cupcake design contest. Let your guests vote for the most creative cupcakes, award prizes to the winners, and encourage everyone to exchange cupcakes with their new friends.

place on top of the bottom-layer cakes. Frost the top-layer cupcakes on all sides.

3. Place chocolate pieces into a small bowl. Dip the cupcakes into the chocolate pieces.

4. Decorate with mint leaves and mint chips.

SESAME CHOCOLATE-COVERED STRAWBERRIES PETIT FOUR CUPCAKES

Many fresh and dried fruits taste great dipped in chocolate. Try dipping mandarin oranges, bananas, grapes, dried apricots, raisins, and dried pineapple. Match the cupcake recipe to the fruit of your choice or create tasty combinations of fruit flavors.

You will need:
Strawberry Cupcakes recipe (page 78)
Strawberry Frosting recipe (page 91)
Sesame chocolate-covered strawberries
Strawberry jam
Dark chocolate bar
Sesame seeds

Mini cupcake pans

1. Prepare the sesame chocolate-covered strawberries by dipping strawberries into melted chocolate and sprinkling sesame seeds on them. Set aside.

2. Spread jam on the tops of the bottom-layer cupcakes.

3. Remove the liners, flip the top-layer cupcakes upside down and place on top of the bottom-layer cakes. Frost the top-layer cupcakes on all sides.

4. Grate a chocolate bar into a small bowl. Add some sesame seeds and stir. Dip the cupcakes into the chocolate mixture.

5. Dip the bottom of the strawberries into the frosting to use it as glue. Place on the cupcake tops.

BLANK CANVAS CUPCAKES

Favorite cupcakes recipe
Sugar Paste Icing (page 91)
Favorite frosting (and color if desired)
Rolling pin
Circle cookie cutter
Pastry bag with decorator tip

1. Bake your favorite recipe and cool the cupcakes.

2. Prepare Sugar Paste Icing. Roll out the icing with a rolling pin. With a circle cookie cutter a little smaller than the diameter of the cupcake, cut the icing into circles and place on the cupcakes.

3. Prepare your favorite frosting. Place in a pastry bag and decorate as you please.

● ● ●

Decorating supplies
Food coloring
Edible markers
Watercolor palettes
Brushes
Pastry bag with star tip
Cookie cutters (for embossing)
Assorted candies

LUAU BEACH PARTY CUPCAKES

Host the ultimate summer bash by serving up these tropical seashore-inspired cupcakes. Made with Piña Colada Cupcakes or Banana Cupcakes, these wonderful flavor and design combinations will add island charm to your next luau.

ALOHA-HULA CUPCAKES

You will need:
Piña Colada Cupcakes recipe (page 73) or Banana Cupcakes recipe (page 50)
Vanilla Frosting recipe (page 92)
Green and blue food coloring
Blue and green colored sugar
Alphabet candy or cereal
Flower candies
Dot candies

1. Divide the frosting into two bowls. Add green food coloring to one batch and blue food coloring to the other.

2. Frost the cupcakes one color in the center and use the other frosting around the perimeter.

3. Sprinkle with colored sugar.

4. Use alphabet cereal to write luau-inspired words like ALOHA and HULA on cupcakes.

5. Using frosting as glue, place small flower candies on top of larger dot candies.

BANANA COCONUT CUPCAKES

You will need:
Banana Cupcakes recipe (page 50)
Banana Coconut Frosting recipe (page 83)
Banana candies or marzipan bananas (see page 42)
Toasted coconut
Green licorice

1. Pour the coconut into a small bowl. Dip frosted cupcakes into the coconut.

2. Overlap the banana candies or marzipan bananas in the cupcake centers to create a bunch.

3. Cut a strand of green licorice and place on banana tops to create stems.

BEACH CUPCAKES

You will need:

Piña Colada Cupcakes (page 73) or Banana Cupcakes recipe (page 50)
Vanilla Frosting recipe (page 92)
Orange and blue food coloring
Graham crackers, crushed
Blue colored sugar
Round candies

Paper umbrella

1. Divide the frosting into three bowls: two equal size batches and one smaller batch. Keep the smallest batch white, and color the other two batches blue and orange with food coloring to resemble water and sand.

2. Spread the blue frosting on one half of each cupcake top. Touch and lift to create peaks that look like waves. Spread the orange frosting on the other halves of the cupcake tops. Create a hilly texture to look like sand. Dip a toothpick into white frosting and add whitecaps to the blue waves.

3. Sprinkle graham crackers over orange frosting to give texture to the sand.

4. Sprinkle blue sugar over blue frosting to make the water sparkle.

5. Place a paper umbrella and a round candy ball on the beach.

Clockwise from top: Fish and Coral Cupcake, Aloha Cupcake, Banana Coconut Cupcake, Sailboat Scene Cupcake, Hula Cupcake, Tiki Head Cupcake. Center: Beach Cupcake.

FISH AND CORAL CUPCAKES

You will need:

Piña Colada Cupcakes (page 73) or Banana Cupcakes recipe (page 50)
Vanilla Frosting recipe (page 92)
Blue food coloring
Green licorice
Blue colored sugar
Fruity cereal
Fish candies

Toothpicks

1. Color the frosting with blue food coloring.
2. Cut the licorice into 1½-inch pointed strips to look like seaweed. Stick the strips into each cupcake in a circle about ½ inch from the perimeter.
3. Sprinkle colored sugar on the frosting on the outside of the seaweed circle.
4. Fill the center of the circle with fruity cereal to look like coral.
5. Stick a toothpick in the bottom of a fish candy. Place the fish in the center of the cupcake.

SAILBOAT SCENE CUPCAKES

You will need:

*Piña Colada Cupcakes recipe (page 73) , Sea Breeze Cupcakes recipe
    (page 76) , or Banana Cupcakes recipe (page 50)*
Vanilla Frosting recipe (page 92)
Orange and blue food coloring
Graham crackers, crushed
Peanut halves
Square candies
Round orange or yellow candies
Orange licorice

1. Divide the frosting into four bowls: two larger batches and two smaller batches. Color the two large batches light sky blue and sand

orange. Keep one of the smaller batches white and color the remaining small batch deep water blue.

2. Spread the orange frosting to cover one-third of each cupcake top. Create a hilly texture to look like sand. Visually dividing the remaining unfrosted space into equal parts, apply deep water blue frosting next to the orange sand and then spread light sky blue frosting across the remaining area. With a toothpick add white frosting to the tips of the waves to make whitecaps, and to the sky to make clouds.

3. Sprinkle graham crackers over orange frosting to texture the sand.

4. To make the sailboat, place a peanut half on the water to look like the keel of a boat. Cut the square candies diagonally to form triangles. These will become sails.

5. To make the sun, place a round orange or yellow candy in the sky. Cut orange licorice into small pieces to make the rays.

TIKI HEAD CUPCAKES

You will need:
Piña Colada Cupcakes (page 73) or Banana Cupcakes recipe (page 50)
Vanilla Frosting recipe (page 92)
Green food coloring
Square candies
Small dot candies
Licorice
Large dot candies

1. Divide the frosting into two bowls. Leave one white and color the other green with food coloring. Reserve a few tablespoons of frosting to use as glue.

2. Frost the cupcake tops white from the center to ½ inch from the perimeter. Frost the perimeters green.

3. Attach four square candies to create tiki heads. Using frosting as glue, attach small dot candies to make faces.

4. Cut licorice and lay across the center. Using frosting as glue attach candy flowers to the licorice. Place a candy dot at the intersection point.

5. Push candy dots into the frosting around the cupcake perimeter.

DINNER PARTY CUPCAKES

These grown-up dinner cupcakes allow you to shine. The recipes are diverse enough that you're bound to find the perfect match for any main course. At a dinner or dessert party you can serve these cupcakes with no liners on a plate drizzled with sauces or in their liners with the sauces drizzled on top.

Clockwise, from top left: Black Bottom Madeleine Cupcake, Chocolate Almond Raspberry Cupcake, Tiramisù Cupcake, Cheesecake Cupcake, Apple à La Mode Cupcake. Center: Napoleon Cupcake

APPLE À LA MODE CUPCAKES

You will need:

Apple Cupcakes recipe (page 50)
Walnut Apple Raisin Topping recipe (page 101)
Caramel Topping recipe (page 95)
Vanilla ice cream

Melon baller

1. With a melon baller, scoop a small amount of vanilla ice cream onto the cupcakes.

2. Pour the Caramel Topping on the plates or over the cupcakes.

3. Top with Walnut Apple Raisin Topping.

BLACK BOTTOM MADELEINE CUPCAKES

You will need:

Black Bottom Cupcakes recipe (page 51)
Rich Chocolate Cupcakes (page 75) or Golden Cupcakes recipe (page 64)
White Chocolate Sauce recipe (page 101)
Dark Chocolate Sauce recipe (page 98)
Cocoa powder
Confectioners' sugar

Madeleine mold
Decorator gel

1. Bake Black Bottom Cupcakes in liners or ungreased cupcake pans. Bake Rich Chocolate or Golden Cupcakes in a Madeleine mold.

2. Prepare the White and Dark Chocolate Sauces. If serving cupcakes on a plate, pour White Chocolate Sauce on half of the plate and Dark Chocolate Sauce on the other half. Place the cupcake on the plate.

3. Using decorator gel, glue a madeleine to each Black Bottom Cupcake.

4. Drizzle White and Dark Chocolate Sauces over the cupcakes.

CHEESECAKE CUPCAKES

There are many variations of cheesecake to enjoy. Here are just a few. Fruit sauces and syrups can either be poured on the cupcake tops or on the plates.

You will need:
Cheesecake Cupcakes recipe (page 54) or variations listed below
Fresh fruit

1. Bake Cheesecake Cupcakes.
2. Top with fresh fruit or toppings of your choice.

Variations

MAPLE WALNUT CHEESECAKE CUPCAKES
Drizzle maple syrup on the plates or over the cupcakes and top with walnuts.

CHOCOLATE CHEESECAKE CUPCAKES
Pour chocolate syrup on the plates or over the cupcakes and top with chocolate chips.

CITRUS CHEESECAKE CUPCAKES
Add 2 tablespoons of citrus zest (orange, lemon, or lime) to the batter before baking. Serve with Orange Sauce (page 100).

RASPBERRY CHOCOLATE CHEESECAKE CUPCAKES
Drizzle the cupcakes or plates with Raspberry Sauce (page 100) and top with grated chocolate.

PECAN CARAMEL CHEESECAKE CUPCAKES
Drizzle Caramel Topping (page 95) on the plates or over the cupcakes. Sprinkle with pecans and chocolate.

WHITE CHOCOLATE STRAWBERRY CHEESECAKE CUPCAKES
Pour Strawberry Sauce (page 101) on a plate or over the cupcakes. Cover with white chocolate chips.

CHOCOLATE ALMOND RASPBERRY CUPCAKES

You will need:

Chocolate Raspberry Cupcakes recipe (page 59)
White Chocolate Buttercream Frosting recipe (page 94)
Raspberry Sauce recipe (page 100)
Whole almonds
Gold leaf
Raspberries

1. Apply thick frosting to the cupcakes.
2. Spoon the Raspberry Sauce on the plates or over the cupcakes.
3. Wrap the almonds with gold leaf. If it doesn't stay on, cover the almonds with frosting to make them sticky.
4. Garnish cupcakes with gold almonds and raspberries.

NAPOLEON CUPCAKES

You will need:

Golden Cupcakes recipe (page 64)
Green, red, and yellow food coloring
Strawberry Sauce recipe (page 101)
Rich Chocolate Frosting recipe (page 90)
Chopped nuts
Strawberries
Chocolate chunks

1. Prepare the cupcake batter. Divide the batter into three equal batches. With food coloring, color one batch green, one red, and one yellow.
2. Fill liners one-third full with red batter. Fill an additional third with yellow batter. These will be your bottom layers.
3. Grease and flour another pan. Fill cups one-third full with the green batter, then another third with red batter. These will be your top layers. Continue filling the liners and pans, alternating the colors. Be sure to use an equal amount of each color. Bake and cool.

4. Spread the Strawberry Sauce on the bottom-layer cupcake tops.

5. Flip the top layers upside down and attach to the bottom layers.

6. Frost the cupcakes.

7. Spoon chopped nuts onto the cupcakes.

8. Garnish with strawberries and chocolate.

TIRAMISÙ CUPCAKES

You will need:

Kahlúa Cupcakes recipe (page 65)

Tiramisù Cream recipe (page 103)

½ cup strong coffee

3 tablespoons Kahlúa

Cocoa powder

Ladyfinger cookies

Chocolate

Snowflake stencil (see page 30)

1. Prepare the cupcake batter. Fill the liners half full with batter and bake. When cupcakes are done, prick holes in the tops with a fork.

2. Combine coffee and Kahlúa. Pour over the cupcakes.

3. Top cupcakes with Tiramisù Cream.

4. Position the snowflake stencil over the cupcakes and sprinkle cocoa powder onto the cupcakes.

5. Garnish with ladyfinger cookies and chocolate.

COCKTAIL PARTY CUPCAKES

These cupcakes put a new spin on popular drink flavors, plus the Rum Syrup gives a sweet bite that cannot be achieved with extracts or nonalcoholic syrups. Serve them as a unique snack for hipster, party-hopping guests.

CHOCOLATE LIQUEUR CUPCAKES

Soaking assorted liqueurs into the cupcakes and adding different liqueurs to the icing customizes these cupcakes.

You will need:
Chocolate Cupcakes recipe (page 58)
Liqueur Icing recipe (page 87)
Favorite liqueurs
Chocolate Curls (see page 39)
Chocolate liqueur-bottle candies

1. Bake the cupcakes and prepare the icing.
2. Prick holes in cupcake tops with a fork. Brush on your favorite liqueur. Ice the cupcakes.
3. Top cupcakes with Chocolate Curls and chocolate liqueur-bottle candies.

KAHLÚA AND CREAM CUPCAKES

You will need:
Kahlúa Cupcakes recipe (page 65)
White Chocolate Buttercream Frosting recipe (page 94)
Kahlúa
Cocoa powder
Chocolate-covered espresso beans
Chocolate cutouts (see page 38)
Cylindrical cookies

Pastry bag with bold writing tip

1. Prick holes in cooled cupcake tops with a fork. Brush on Kahlúa.

2. Fill the pastry bag with frosting. Make bold lines with the frosting.

3. Sprinkle cocoa on the cupcakes.

4. Top with chocolate-covered espresso beans, chocolate cutouts, and cylindrical cookies.

PIÑA COLADA CUPCAKES

You will need:

Piña Colada Cupcakes recipe (page 73)
Toasted Coconut Cream Cheese Frosting recipe (page 92)
Rum Syrup recipe (page 100)
Toasted coconut (page 46)
Pineapple Maraschino Cherry Kabobs (page 47)

1. Prick holes in the tops of cupcakes with a fork. With a brush or a tablespoon, douse cupcakes with Rum Syrup.

2. Frost the cupcakes.

3. Pour the coconut into a small bowl. Dip the freshly frosted cupcakes into the toasted coconut.

4. Garnish with Pineapple Maraschino Cherry Kabobs.

SCREWDRIVER CUPCAKES

You will need:

Orange Cupcakes recipe (page 76)
Spiked Orange Frosting recipe (page 91)
Orange liqueur (Grand Marnier, Triple Sec, curaçao)
Orange colored sugar
Candied Citrus Peel (page 94)
Orange Slices and Maraschino Cherries (page 46)

1. Prick holes in cupcake tops with a fork. Brush on orange liqueur.

Back row: Chocolate Liqueur Cupcake, Kahlúa and Cream Cupcake, Piña Colada Cupcake. Front row: Screwdriver Cupcake, Sea Breeze Cupcake, Strawberry Daquiri Cupcake.

2. Frost the cupcakes and sprinkle with orange sugar and Candied Citrus Peel.

3. Place Orange Slices and Maraschino Cherries on the cupcakes.

SEA BREEZE CUPCAKES

You will need:

Sea Breeze Cupcakes recipe (page 76)
Rum Syrup recipe (page 100)
Lime Icing recipe (page 87)
Green colored sugar
Cranberries (dried or fresh)
Lime slices (page 46)
Candied Citrus Peel (page 94)

1. Prick holes in cupcake tops with a fork. Brush on Rum Syrup.

2. Frost the cupcakes and sprinkle with green sugar.

3. Garnish with cranberries, lime wedges, and Candied Citrus Peel.

STRAWBERRY DAIQUIRI CUPCAKES

You will need:

Strawberry Lime Cupcakes recipe (page 78)
Rum Syrup recipe (page 100)
Strawberry Frosting recipe (page 91)
Red food coloring
Red colored sugar
Mint Strawberries (page 47)

1. Prick holes in the tops of cupcakes with a fork. With a brush or a tablespoon, douse the cupcakes with Rum Syrup.

2. Color the frosting with red food coloring. Frost the cupcakes and sprinkle with red sugar.

3. Place Mint Strawberries on cupcake tops.

OFFICE PARTY/COFFEE BREAK CUPCAKES

Celebrations at the office are always welcome. Take a coffee break and share some social time with your coworkers. Cupcakes are great for office gatherings because they are portable, easy to share, and neat. You might choose to frost or top the cupcakes when you get to the office to make them look extra fresh.

CARAMEL MOCHA CUPCAKES

You will need:
  Mocha Cupcakes recipe (page 69)
  Whipped Cream recipe (page 93)
  Caramel Topping recipe (page 95)
  Chocolate-covered espresso beans
  Chocolate Curls (see page 39)

1. Top the cupcakes with Whipped Cream.
2. Drizzle Caramel Topping in a pattern on cupcake tops.
3. Sprinkle on chocolate-covered espresso beans.
4. Garnish with Chocolate Curls.

COFFEE AND CREAM CUPCAKES

You will need:
  Coffee Cupcakes recipe (page 60)
  Pastry Cream recipe (page 102)
  Coffee Cream Cheese Frosting recipe (page 85)
  Turbinado sugar
  Espresso beans

  Pastry bag with large tip

1. With a grapefruit spoon, remove two teaspoons of cake in a cone shape from the center of each cupcake. Save the removed cake. With a pastry bag or spoon, fill each hole with Pastry Cream. Replace the cake cone.

2. Place the frosting in a pastry bag. Create a spiral shape with the frosting, starting at the perimeter and working your way toward the center.

3. Sprinkle on turbinado sugar (it is only partially refined and yellowish in color).

4. Top with espresso beans.

HAZELNUT COFFEE CUPCAKES

You will need:
> *Chopped hazelnuts*
> *Hazelnut Coffee Cupcakes recipe (page 60)*
> *Coffee Cream Cheese Frosting recipe (page 85)*
> *Chocolate-covered hazelnuts (page 39)*

1. Pour chopped hazelnuts into a bowl. Dip cupcakes into the hazelnuts.

2. After frosting cupcakes, place a whole chocolate-covered hazelnut in the center of each cupcake top.

JAVA CHIP CUPCAKES

You will need:
> *Java Chip Cupcakes recipe (page 60)*
> *Mocha Frosting recipe (page 89)*
> *Mocha Sauce recipe (page 99)*
> *Chocolate shapes (see page 38)*

1. Apply thick frosting around the perimeter of cooled cupcakes. Leave a reservoir in the center. Pour Mocha Sauce into the reservoir.

2. Top with the chocolate shapes.

MOCHA CUPCAKES

You will need:
> *Mocha Cupcakes recipe (page 69)*
> *Mocha Frosting recipe (page 89)*
> *Grated chocolate*
> *Chocolate-covered espresso beans*
>
> *Circle stencil (see Chapter 9)*

1. Place stencil lightly on frosted cupcake tops. Dust grated chocolate over the cupcakes, then lift the stencil away.

2. Top with chocolate-covered espresso beans.

Back row, left to right: Peppermint Mocha Cupcake, Hazelnut Coffee Cupcake, Java Chip Cupcake. Front row, left to right: Mocha Cupcake, Caramel Mocha Cupcake, Coffee and Cream Cupcake

PEPPERMINT MOCHA CUPCAKES

You will need:
 Peppermint candies
 Melted chocolate
 Peppermint Mocha Cupcakes recipe (page 69)
 Mocha Frosting recipe (page 89)

1. Dip peppermint candies in melted chocolate.
2. Top frosted cupcakes chocolate-covered peppermint candies.

TV PARTY CUPCAKES

Whether you're watching the big game or celebrities walk the red carpet, fun-themed cupcakes and friendly bonding in front of the TV go hand in hand. These cupcakes can also be made to celebrate your family champion or star's big win.

ACADEMY AWARDS PARTY CUPCAKES

You will need:
 Corn Cupcakes recipe (page 61)
 Browned Butter Icing recipe (page 83)
 Popcorn
 Melted butter
 Star-shaped candies (assorted sizes)

 White glue, or tape
 Gold paper
 Toothpick

1. Ice the cupcakes, reserving some icing as glue.
2. Top the cupcakes with popcorn, using the frosting as glue to make tall piles on each one. Drizzle melted butter over poporn with a spoon.
3. Attach candy stars to the popcorn using frosting as glue.
4. Make Oscar statues out of gold paper and glue them to toothpicks. Place the statues on top of the popcorn piles.

ALL-NIGHT TV PARTY CUPCAKES

You will need:
Brownie Cupcakes recipe (page 52)
Favorite frosting recipe
Mini peanut butter cups
Chocolate candy rolls
White chocolate chips

Mini cupcake pan

1. Bake an equal number of mini- and regular-sized cupcakes; let cool. Attach a mini cupcake to the top of each regular-sized cupcake with frosting. Frost the double-tiered cupcakes.

2. Center an unwrapped mini peanut butter cup on top of each cupcake.

3. Cut chocolate rolls in half. Place in a standing position around each peanut butter cup.

4. Using frosting as glue, attach white chocolate chips to the tops of the candy roll pieces and the mini cupcakes.

OLYMPICS PARTY CUPCAKES

You will need:
Chocolate Beer Cupcakes recipe (page 55) or favorite cupcake recipe
Vanilla Frosting recipe (page 92), doubled
Yellow food coloring
Colored dot candies (blue, black, red, yellow, and green)
Colored sugar (blue, black, red, yellow, and green)

Pastry bag with small writing tip

1. Divide the frosting into two batches, one large and one small. Color the small batch with yellow food coloring. Frost the cupcakes white.

2. Fill a pastry bag with yellow and pipe the Olympic rings on each cupcake. If you like, write the year and location of the Olympics on the cupcakes.

4. Sprinkle rings with Olympic-colored sugar.

5. Place Olympic-colored dot candies around the perimeter.

Clockwise, from top: Academy Awards Party Cupcake, World Series Party Cupcake, All-Night TV Party Cupcake, Olympics Party Cupcake, Super Bowl Party Cupcake.

SUPER BOWL PARTY CUPCAKES

You will need:

Chocolate Beer Cupcakes (page 55), or Root Beer Cupcakes (page 63), or Chocolate Cupcakes recipe (page 58)

Vanilla Frosting recipe (page 92)

Food coloring

Colored sugars

Football candies

Toothpicks

More Party Cupcakes

Poker and Bridge Card Party Cupcakes

Bake your favorite cupcakes and prepare your favorite frosting. Place mixed nuts on top. Tape small playing cards to toothpicks and place in cupcakes.

Bon Voyage Party Cupcakes

Bake your favorite cupcakes and prepare your favorite frosting. To make frosting waves, refer to page 29; to make a sky, refer to page 29. To make a road, use black frosting with yellow candies as the line Top with a transportation toy or a candy airplane, boat, or car.

Housewarming/Block Party

Build a house using technique on page 152. Decorate it to look like your new house for a housewarming or the houses in your neighborhood.

1. Prepare the frosting and divide into two bowls. Color each batch your favorite team's colors with food coloring.

2. Frost the center of the cupcake one color and use the other color around the perimeter.

3. Sprinkle with colored sugars that match your team's colors.

4. Insert toothpicks into football candies.

5. Insert into cupcakes.

WORLD SERIES PARTY CUPCAKES

You will need:

Chocolate Beer Cupcakes (page 55) or Chocolate Cupcakes recipe (page 58)
Vanilla Frosting recipe (page 92)
Red string licorice
Candy baseballs

Paper
Glue
Toothpicks

1. Cut red licorice into two long strips and several 1/4-inch small strips. Assemble on the frosted cupcakes to look like the seams on a baseball.

2. Make a flag: Draw your favorite team's logo on a small piece of paper. Glue the edge of the paper to a toothpick. Place the flag on the cupcake.

3. Top the cupcakes with candy baseballs and gloves.

Holidays

CHRISTMAS CUPCAKES

Christmas is more than just a day. It is a season synonymous with baking and filled with exciting preparations. The many celebrations offer us plenty of opportunities to bake these merry holiday cupcakes. Enjoy them when you invite guests to decorate a Christmas tree, host a family gathering, or need to leave a treat for Santa.

EGGNOG CUPCAKES

You will need:

Eggnog Cupcakes recipe (page 63)
Cinnamon Whipped Cream recipe (page 93)
Rum Syrup recipe (page 100)
Ground cinnamon
Cinnamon sticks
Cinnamon imperials
Christmas tree candies

1. Brush 1–2 tablespoons of Rum Syrup over each cupcake.
2. Spoon on the cinnamon Whipped Cream.

Clockwise, from top: Gingerbread House Cupcake, Gingerbread Man Cupcake, Eggnog Cupcake, Peppermint Candy Candy Cupcake. On tabletop: North Pole Cupcake.

3. Sprinkle with ground cinnamon.

4. Garnish with a cinnamon stick and cinnamon imperials. To make holly berries: Place two mini Christmas tree candies next to cinnamon imperials.

GINGERBREAD HOUSE CUPCAKES

You will need:

Gingerbread Cupcakes recipe (page 64)
Ginger Cream Cheese Frosting recipe (page 86)
Shredded coconut
Graham crackers
Holiday candies (Santas, peppermints, cinnamon imperials, candy stars, etc.)
Christmas tree candies

1. Pour the shredded coconut into a small bowl. Dip the frosted cupcakes into the coconut.

2. To build a house, use graham cracker pieces to make the four walls and the roof. Using frosting as glue, glue the house together. Decorate the house exterior with candy. Place on the cupcake.

3. Place Christmas trees and other holiday candies around the house.

GINGERBREAD MEN CUPCAKES

You will need:

Gingerbread Cupcakes recipe (page 64)
Ginger Cream Cheese Frosting recipe (page 86)
Gingerbread Men Cookies recipe (page 98)
Gumdrops
Holiday candies

1. Attach decorated Gingerbread Men Cookies to frosted Gingerbread Cupcakes, either standing up or lying down.

2. Decorate cupcake perimeters with gumdrops and holiday candies.

NORTH POLE CUPCAKES

You will need:

Spice Cupcakes recipe (page 77)
Cream Cheese Frosting recipe (page 86)
Marzipan Snowmen (see page 45)
Flaked coconut
Candy cane sticks
Red candy dots

1. Pour the flaked coconut into a small bowl. Dip the frosted cupcakes into the coconut.

2. Using frosting as glue, attach a Marzipan snowman to each cupcake.

3. Place a candy cane stick in each cupcake. Top with a red candy dot using frosting as glue.

PEPPERMINT CANDY CANE CUPCAKES

You will need:

Peppermint Cupcakes (page 73)
Peppermint Cream Cheese Frosting (page 86)
White chocolate chunks
Peppermint candies, assorted shapes

1. Top the frosted cupcakes with white chocolate chunks and whole and crushed peppermint candies.

NEW YEAR'S EVE CUPCAKES

What could be more worthy of celebration than starting a new year? New Year's Eve reminds us of the past, yet holds hope for the future. Ring in the new year with these Champagne Cupcakes and stay awake extra late with Midnight Mocha Cupcakes.

CHAMPAGNE CUPCAKES

You will need:
> *Champagne Cupcakes recipe (page 53)*
> *Champagne Buttercream Icing recipe (page 84)*
> *Champagne*
> *Chocolate champagne-bottle candies*
> *Silver candy dots*

1. Brush 1 tablespoon of champagne on the top of each baked cupcake. Ice the cupcakes.
2. Top with chocolate champagne-bottle candies.
3. Decorate with silver candy dots to look like champagne bubbles.

MIDNIGHT MOCHA CUPCAKES

You will need:
> *Mocha Cupcakes recipe (page 69)*
> *Vanilla Frosting recipe (page 92)*
> *Food coloring*
> *Chocolate-covered espresso beans*
> *Chocolate bar*
> *Candy dots*

1. Divide the frosting into two batches. Make each batch a different color with food coloring.
2. Frost the cupcakes in the center with one color and around the perimeter with the other color.
3. Place twelve chocolate-covered espresso beans on the cupcake, like numbers on a clock.

Clockwise, from top, right: Champagne Cupcake, New Year's Baby Cupcake, New Year Cupcake, Midnight Mocha Cupcake, Center: Times Square Cupcake

4. With a knife, cut a chocolate bar to make clock hands. Place hands on the cupcakes pointing at twelve o'clock. Place a candy dot in the center where the hands meet.

NEW YEAR CUPCAKES

You will need:
> *Champagne Cupcakes recipe (page 53)*
> *Champagne Buttercream Icing recipe (page 84)*
> *Food coloring*
> *Nonpareils*
> *Colored sugars*
>
> *Pastry bag with writing tip*

1. Divide the frosting into two bowls. Color each a different color. Frost the cupcakes with one batch.

2. Pour the nonpareils into a small bowl. Dip the edges of cupcakes into the nonpareils.

3. Sprinkle colored sugars on cupcake centers.

4. Place the second color of frosting in a pastry bag with a writing tip. Write the year and make dots and stripes around the perimeter with frosting.

NEW YEAR'S BABY CUPCAKES

You will need:
> *Champagne*
> *Champagne Cupcakes recipe (page 53)*
> *Champagne Buttercream Icing recipe (page 84)*
> *Colored sugar*
> *Chocolate taffy*
> *Candy dots*
>
> *White paper*
> *Glue*
> *Toy baby*

1. Brush 1 tablespoon of champagne on each cupcake top. Ice the cupcakes.

2. Sprinkle with colored sugar.

3. Coil chocolate taffy into a spiral on cupcake tops.

4. Write the year on a small piece a paper and glue it to the toy baby. Make a cone-shaped paper hat for the baby. Glue a candy dot to the tip of the hat.

5. Place the New Year's baby in the center of the spiral.

TIMES SQUARE CUPCAKES

You will need:

Champagne Cupcakes recipe (page 53)
Champagne Buttercream Icing recipe (page 84)
Sugar crystals
Wrapped candy or plastic balls
Assorted candies

Bamboo skewerss
Ribbon

1. Pour the sugar crystals into a small bowl. Dip the frosted cupcakes into the sugar.

2. Write the year on the outside of a wrapped candy or plastic ball. Attach the ball to a bamboo skewer wrapped in ribbon. Stick into cupcake.

3. Place assorted candies on the cupcakes..

VALENTINE'S DAY CUPCAKES

Valentine's Day is the perfect time to show all of our friends and lovers a little appreciation. Tokens of our affection, such as these delicious Valentine cupcakes make the perfect gift for lovebirds, friends, and children. As seductive as a box of chocolate, these homemade cupcakes are straight from the heart.

CHERRY CORDIAL CUPCAKES

You will need:

Cherry Cordial Cupcakes recipe (page 55)
Dark Chocolate Icing recipe (page 86)
Grated chocolate bar
Cherry truffle candies
Small candy hearts
Chocolate nonpareils

Optional:
Plastic cupcake packaging
Ribbon

1. Grate a chocolate bar into a small bowl. Dip the perimeters of the frosted cupcakes into the grated chocolate.

2. Place a cherry truffle candy in the center of each cupcake top. With frosting, glue a candy heart to each cherry truffle top.

3. Surround the base of the cherry truffle with chocolate nonpareils.

4. Place the cupcakes in plastic cupcake containers. Tie them with bows and give them out as Valentine treats.

ROSES AND TRUFFLES CUPCAKES

You will need:

Chocolate Cupcakes recipe (page 58)
Rosewater Icing recipe (page 90)
Chocolate truffles
Red and pink colored sugars
Marzipan roses (page 44)
Small candy hearts

Red cellophane
Ribbon

1. Submerge a chocolate truffle into each batter-filled cupcake liner before baking. Bake, cool, and frost.

2. Sprinkle the cupcakes with red and pink colored sugars.

Clockwise, from top: Roses and Truffles Cupcake, Cherry Cordial Cupcake, Stacked Hearts Cupcake, Strawberry Valentine Card Cupcake.

3. Place marzipan roses on cupcake tops.

4. Wrap cupcakes in red cellophane and tie with ribbon. Give them out to friends with love in your heart.

STACKED HEARTS CUPCAKES

You will need:

Golden Cupcakes recipe (page 64)
Vanilla Frosting recipe (page 92)
Red food coloring
Large candy hearts
Medium candy hearts
Small candy hearts
Candy-coated licorice (white)

1. Color the frosting red with food coloring. Reserve a few tablespoons of frosting to use as glue. Frost the cupcakes.

2. Using frosting as glue, place a large candy heart in the center of each cupcake. Then attach a smaller heart on top and repeat with a third, even smaller, heart.

4. Radiate pieces of candy-coated licorice from the heart.

STRAWBERRY VALENTINE CARD CUPCAKES

You will need:

Strawberry Cupcakes recipe (page 78)
Strawberry Frosting recipe (page 91)
Chocolate candy
Red food coloring
Strawberry candies

Card stock
White glue or tape
Curved straws

1. Submerge a chocolate candy into batter-filled cupcake liners before baking. Bake and cool.

2. Divide the frosting into two small bowls. Color one batch an even brighter red with red food coloring and leave the other half as is.

3. Frost the cupcakes with uncolored frosting in the middle and brighter red frosting around the perimeter.

4. Outline the edges with strawberry candies.

5. Make Valentine cards out of card stock. Tape or glue cards to curvy straws. Stick cards into the cupcake centers.

EASTER CUPCAKES

On Easter morning bunnies, eggs, candy, and flowers abound—let them inspire you! Prepare these cupcakes with Low-Fat Carrot or Lemon Cupcakes—traditional flavors for this holiday. Use festive candies that are available only at this time of the year.

BOUNTIFUL EGGS CUPCAKES

You will need:
Low-Fat Carrot Cupcakes recipe (page 67)
Cream Cheese Frosting recipe (page 86)
Green food coloring
Green colored sugar
Jelly beans
Gummy candy flowers

Small plastic eggs that split into two pieces

1. Color the frosting green with food coloring. Frost the cupcakes.

2. Sprinkle with green sugar.

3. Fill the plastic eggs with jelly beans and either close the eggs for a surprise or keep the eggs open to display their treats. Attach eggs to the center of cupcake tops.

4. Radiate gummy candy flowers around the eggs.

Counterclockwise, from top left: Chocolate Egg Cupcake, Dozen Eggs Cupcake, Lemon Flowers Cupcake, Lemon Marshmallow Bunnies Cupcake, Carrot Cake Cupcake. Center: Bountiful Eggs Cupcake.

CARROT CAKE CUPCAKES

You will need:

    Low-Fat Carrot Cupcake recipe (page 67)

    Cream Cheese Frosting recipe (page 86)

    Chopped walnuts

    Marzipan carrots (see page 43)

1. Pour chopped walnuts into a small bowl. Dip the frosted cupcakes into the nuts.

2. Place a marzipan carrot in the center of each cupcake top.

CHOCOLATE EGG CUPCAKES

You will need:

Chocolate Carrot Cupcakes recipe (page 56)
Chocolate Frosting recipe (page 84)
Rice Cereal Topping recipe (page 100)
Nonpareils
Large chocolate candy eggs
Candy flowers
Candy dots
Colored decorator gel

1. Prepare the frosting. Reserve some to use as glue. Frost the cupcakes.

2. Spoon the Rice Cereal Topping onto each frosted cupcake to look like a nest. Attach candy dots to the nest with frosting.

3. Cover each chocolate egg with frosting. Pour nonpareils into a bowl and dip frosted eggs into nonpareils. Attach candy dots and flowers to eggs with frosting. Place each candy egg in the nests.

4. If desired, outline additional patterns on the egg with colored decorator gel. Experiment with different toppings and patterns in decorating the chocolate eggs.

DOZEN EGGS CUPCAKES

You will need:

Low-Fat Carrot Cupcakes recipe (page 67)
Cream Cheese Frosting recipe (page 86)
Green food coloring
Green shredded coconut (page 22)
Candy flowers
Candy eggs

1. Color the frosting green with food coloring. Reserve some frosting to use as glue. Frost the cupcakes.

2. Pour the coconut into a small bowl. Dip the cupcakes into the coconut.

3. Sprinkle the tops with candy flowers.

4. Using frosting as glue, attach a dozen candy eggs to each cupcake top.

LEMON FLOWERS CUPCAKES

You will need:

Lemon Cupcakes recipe (page 66)
Cream Cheese Frosting recipe (page 86)
Food coloring
Jelly beans
Candy flowers

1. Divide the frosting into several bowls. Color the frosting in springtime pastel colors with food coloring. Frost the cupcakes using one color in the center and another color around the perimeter.

2. Place a jelly bean in the center of each cupcake top. Radiate petals around the jelly bean.

3. Scatter smaller candy flowers around the perimeters.

LEMON MARSHMALLOW BUNNIES CUPCAKES

You will need:

Lemon Cupcakes recipe (page 66)
Marshmallow Frosting recipe (page 89)
Marshmallow bunnies
Green string licorice

1. Place marshmallow bunnies on frosted cupcake tops.

2. Cut green string licorice into small pieces to look like blades of grass. Place the licorice around the bunnies.

FOURTH OF JULY CUPCAKES

Oh, say can you see these wonderful cupcakes! Americans love to celebrate on the Fourth with picnics, block parties, and barbecues. What better time to—you guessed it—bake cupcakes? Anything goes when it's colored red, white, and blue, or with stars and stripes.

BAM-POW-KABOOM CUPCAKES

You will need:
 Strawberry Cupcakes recipe (page 78)
 Cream Cheese Frosting recipe (page 86)
 Candy letters
 Red, white, and blue oval fruit candies
 Candy stars
 Colored sugar

1. Sprinkle the frosted cupcakes with colored sugar.
2. With candy letters write your favorite exploding words like BAM, POW, and KABOOM.
3. Radiate oval fruit candies from the word.
4. Using frosting as glue, attach candy stars to the oval candies.

BBQ/PICNIC CUPCAKES

You will need:
 Chocolate Cupcakes recipe (page 58)
 Vanilla Frosting recipe (page 92)
 Green coconut
 Mini marshmallows
 Red licorice
 Hamburger and hot dog candles

1. Reserve some frosting to use as glue. Frost the cupcakes.
2. Pour green coconut into a bowl and dip the frosted cupcakes into the coconut to make the grass.

3. Cut the red licorice into the same-sized pieces as the mini marshmallows. Using frosting as glue, attach them to the cupcake, alternating pieces to make a red and white checkered picnic blanket.

4. Glue the hamburger and hot dog candies to the picnic blanket.

NOTE: If you cannot find hamburger and hot dog candies, you can make a hamburger out of two round cookies, spreading chocolate frosting in the middle and sesame seeds on top. Hamburgers and hot dogs can also be made out of marzipan.

BLUEBERRY RASPBERRY CREAM CHEESE CUPCAKES

You will need:

Blueberry Raspberry Cupcakes recipe (page 52)
Cream Cheese Frosting recipe (page 86)
Red and blue food coloring, optional
Blueberries
Raspberries
Candy stars

1. Divide the frosting into three small bowls. Crush the blueberries into one batch to color it blue, crush raspberries into another batch to color it red. Leave the third batch white. For brighter colors add a few drops of red and blue food coloring.

2. Frost the cupcakes with the three colors in a bull's-eye pattern.

3. Top with blueberries, raspberries, and candy stars.

FIREWORKS CUPCAKES

You will need:

White Cupcakes recipe (page 81)
Vanilla Frosting recipe (page 92)
Red and blue food coloring
Fizzing rock candies
Alphabet candy
Candy stars

Party toothpicks

Clockwise, from top: Flag Cupcake,
Blueberry Raspberry Cream Cheese Cupcake,
Bam-Pow-Kaboom Cupcake, BBQ/Picnic
Cupcake, Red, White, and Blue Cupcake.
On napkins: Fireworks Cupcake

1. Divide the cupcake batter into thirds. Color one batch red, one batch blue, and leave one white.

2. Pour a few tablespoons of each batter into cupcake liners until they are two-thirds full. With a knife swirl the colors slightly to marbleize. Bake, cool, and frost.

3. Sprinkle fizzing rock candies on cupcakes.

4. Place the alphabet candy letters USA in the center of the cupcakes.

5. Place candy stars around the perimeters.

6. Decorate with party toothpicks to look like exploding fireworks.

FLAG CUPCAKES

You will need:

White Cupcakes recipe (page 81)
Marshmallow Frosting recipe (page 89)
1 cup red and blue soft candies, chopped, plus more for decorating
1 cup mini marshmallows, chopped, plus more for decorating
Star candies
Colored sugar

Mini flags

1. Mix red and blue candies and marshmallows into the batter-filled cupcakes liners. Bake, cool, and frost cupcakes.

2. Pile more of the mini marshmallows on frosted cupcake tops. Stick mini flags in the centers.

3. Cut more red and blue candies into pieces. Using frosting as glue, cap the marshmallows off with red and blue candies, and star candies, and colored sugar.

RED, WHITE, AND BLUE CUPCAKES

You will need:

White Cupcakes recipe (page 81)
Red and blue food coloring
Vanilla Frosting recipe (page 92)
Blue colored sugar
Star candies
White and colored sprinkles

1. Prepare the cupcake batter. Divide the batter into thirds. With food coloring, color one batch red, and one batch blue. Leave the remaining batch white.

2. Fill cupcakes liners one-quarter full with red batter. Top with white batter until half full. Finally top with blue batter until three-quarters full. Bake and cool.

3. Color the frosting dark blue with food coloring. Frost the cupcakes.

4. Sprinkle blue sugar on cupcakes to make the night sky twinkle. Make stars in the sky with star-shaped candies. Radiate white sprinkles from the stars to make them look like they are exploding. Form clusters of colored sprinkles to look like fireworks.

HALLOWEEN CUPCAKES

There is no such thing as too many Halloween treats. Make your jack-o'-lantern smile with cupcakes!

CARAMEL APPLE CUPCAKES

You will need:
Caramel Apple Cupcakes recipe (page 53)
Ginger Cream Cheese Frosting recipe (page 86)
Caramel Topping recipe (page 94)
Dried apples, cut into pieces
Caramel square

1. Generously frost the cupcakes. Make reservoirs in the frosting centers with a spoon to hold the Caramel Topping. Spoon the topping into the reservoirs.

2. Radiate dried apple pieces from the centers of the cupcakes.

3. Place a caramel square in each center.

JACK-O'-LANTERN CUPCAKES

You will need:
Pumpkin Cupcakes recipe (page 74)
Chocolate Frosting recipe (page 84)
Vanilla Frosting recipe (page 92)
Orange food coloring
Black coloring gel
Orange colored sugar

1. Color Vanilla Frosting orange with food coloring. Color the Chocolate Frosting black with coloring gel.

2. Frost the cooled cupcakes with orange frosting.

3. Sprinkle with orange colored sugar.

4. With a knife, rough out jack-o'-lantern faces with black frosting. Clean up the edges with a toothpick. Make different faces on each cupcake.

MARSHMALLOW GHOST CUPCAKES

You will need:
White Cupcakes recipe (page 81)
Marshmallow Frosting recipe (page 89)
Mini marshmallows
Black sprinkles
Marshmallow ghosts
Candy bats

1. Fill the cupcakes liners two-thirds full with cupcake batter. Submerge a few mini marshmallows in the batter. Bake, cool, and frost.

2. Pour black sprinkles in a small bowl. Dip cupcake perimeters into the sprinkles.

3. Place marshmallow ghosts in the cupcake centers. Place additional mini marshmallows around the perimeters. Using frosting as glue, top mini marshmallows with candy bats.

Clockwise, from top: Caramel Apple Cupcake, Haunted House Cupcake, Jack-o'-Lantern Cupcake, Skeleton Cupcake, Marshmallow Ghost Cupcake. Center: Pumpkin Patch Cupcake

PUMPKIN PATCH CUPCAKES

You will need:
> *Pumpkin Cupcakes recipe (page 74)*
> *Maple Cream Cheese Frosting recipe (page 86)*
> *Green food coloring*
> *Green colored sugar*
> *Candy pumpkins*
> *Orange candy dots*

1. Color the frosting green with food coloring. Frost the cooled cupcakes.

2. Sprinkle green sugar on the cupcakes.

3. Top with candy pumpkins and orange candy dots.

SKELETON CUPCAKES

You will need:
> *Chocolate Cupcakes recipe (page 58)*
> *Chocolate Frosting recipe (page 84)*
> *Black coloring gel*
> *Orange nonpareils*
> *Skeleton tart candies*
> *Orange candy flowers*

1. Color the frosting black with coloring gel. Frost the cupcakes.

2. Pour nonpareils into a small bowl. Dip the perimeters of the cupcakes into the nonpareils.

3. Place tart candies on cupcakes to form skeletons.

4. Fill in remaining spaces with candy flowers.

HAUNTED HOUSE CUPCAKES

You will need:
> *Favorite cupcakes recipe*
> *Vanilla Frosting recipe (page 92)*
> *Green food coloring*

Black decorating gel
Colored sugar
Caramel squares
Graham crackers or wafer cookies, cut into 1-by-1-inch pieces
Small candies in assorted shapes
Black string licorice
Candy corn

Toothpicks or candies
Edible markers
Candy bat

1. Reserve some frosting to use as glue. Divide the remaining frosting into two small bowls. Color one batch black with gel, and color the other green with food coloring.

2. Frost the cupcake green to make the grass. Sprinkle it with colored sugar. Create the sidewalk out of black string licorice.

3. Write RIP on toothpicks to create tombstones and stick them into the grass. The edible alternative is to use an edible marker to write RIP on small candies and place them on the grass.

4. To make the house: Use frosting to glue a candy caramel to the cupcake. Piece the two cracker or cookie squares into a peaked shape with black frosting. Attach the "roof" to the caramel. Cover roof with frosting. Attach small pieces of candy to the caramel to make the doors and windows.

5. Surround the house with candy corn. Attach a candy bat to the candy corn with frosting.

THANKSGIVING CUPCAKES

Thanksgiving is the most anticipated feast of the year for many Americans. It is a time to reflect and get together with friends and family. Here are a variety of cupcake recipes, inspired by the flavors and images of the season, to accommodate the tastes of your many guests. Celebrate your bounty by baking a batch for your favorite local charity, food mission, or homeless shelter.

Clockwise, from top: Maple Fall Leaves Cupcake, Turkey and Cranberry Cupcake, Pumpkin Cupcake. On tabletop: Pecan Pie Cupcake.

MAPLE FALL LEAVES CUPCAKES

You will need:

Maple Walnut Cupcakes recipe (page 68)
Maple Cream Cheese Frosting recipe (page 86)
Maple syrup
Walnut halves
Candy leaves

1. Bake and cool cupcakes. Generously frost. With a spoon make a reservoir in the frosting of each one. Pour a tablespoon of maple syrup into each reservoir.
2. Place walnut halves around maple syrup centers.
3. Sprinkle on candy leaves.

PECAN PIE CUPCAKES

You will need:

Pecan Pie Cupcakes recipe (page 72)
Chocolate-covered pecan halves (page 39)

1. Bake, then cool cupcakes.
2. Place chocolate-covered pecan halves on cupcake tops to decorate.

PUMPKIN CUPCAKES

Pumpkin Cupcakes recipe (page 74)
Cinnamon Whipped Cream recipe (page 93)
Orange food coloring
Marzipan pumpkins (page 43)

1. Bake, cool, and frost cupcakes.
2. Color the Cinnamon Whipped Cream with orange food coloring. Spoon cream onto the cupcake tops. Top with marzipan pumpkins.

TURKEY AND CRANBERRY CUPCAKES

You will need:
Cranberry Cupcakes recipe (page 52)
Dark Chocolate Icing recipe (page 86)
Graham crackers, crushed
Dried cranberries
Marzipan turkey (page 45)

1. Place crushed graham crackers in a small bowl. Dip the cupcakes into the graham crackers.

2. Place marzipan turkey in the center of each cupcake.

3. Decorate with dried cranberries around the perimeter.

CULTURAL HOLIDAYS CUPCAKES

Whether you belong to these cultural groups or just enjoy learning about and celebrating other cultures, these cupcakes will get you started. Though the Hanukkah and Passover recipes may not be kosher, they're still a yummy way to celebrate Jewish culture.

CHINESE NEW YEAR CUPCAKES

Chinese New Year is celebrated as a fifteen-day family affair, a time of reunion and thanksgiving. The celebration includes a religious ceremony honoring Heaven and Earth and the family ancestors. Traditionally Moon Cakes are eaten on Chinese New Year because the Chinese New Year is based on the lunar calendar. These Moon Cupcakes are decorated with crescent moons. Another alternative is to top each cupcake with a Chinese fortune cookie.

You will need:
Golden Cupcakes recipe (page 64)
Vanilla Frosting recipe (page 92)
Blue food coloring
Candy stars

Pastry bag with writing tip
Glue
Toothpick
Animal images fromChinese zodiac (dragon, rabbit, ram, etc.)

1. Bake and cool cupcakes. Divide the frosting into two batches, leaving one batch white and coloring the other dark blue.
2. Reserve some white frosting to write the year. Using a small knife, make a crescent moon with white frosting on each cupcake top. Use blue frosting to make night skies.
3. Fill a pastry bag with white frosting and write the year in the blue skies.
4. Place candy stars in the skies.

Clockwise, from top, left: St.Patrick's Day Cupcake, Chinese New Year Cupcake, Mardi Gras Cupcake, Cinco de Mayo Cupcake. Center: Passover Cupcake

5. Glue Chinese zodiac animal images, depending on the year, onto toothpicks. Place them on the cupcakes.

CINCO DE MAYO CUPCAKES

Cinco de Mayo, the fifth of May, commemorates the victory of the Mexicans over the French army at the Battle of Puebla in 1862. It is a popular holiday in the American Southwest. Tres leches ("three-milk cake") became a popular dessert in Mexico and a special dessert for parties. Enjoy this simpler cupcake version at your next fiesta.

You will need:
    Tres Leches Cupcakes recipe (page 79)
    Whipped Cream recipe (page 93)
    Red and green colored sugar
    Mint leaves
    Strawberries

    Small Mexican flags

1. Bake and cool cupcakes. Frost with Whipped Cream, then sprinkle one side of cupcake tops with green sugar and the other side with red sugar.
2. Place mint leaves and strawberry in the center of each cupcake.
3. Garnish with a flag.

HANUKKAH CUPCAKES

Hanukkah, also known as the Festival of Lights, commemorates the victory of the Jews over the Hellenistic Syrians in the year 165 B.C.E. Hanukkah is celebrated for eight days and usually occurs in December. Jews light menorahs from the shamus (center, taller candle) one candle at a time each night for eight days. This cupcake menorah is a great way to celebrate the final day of Hannukkah.

You will need:

    Chocolate Chip Cinnamon Cupcakes recipe (page 56)
    Vanilla Frosting recipe (page 92)
    Blue sugar
    Hanukkah candies or toy dreidls
    Candles

1. Make one double-layer cupcake as the shamus: Place one cupcake upside down on top of another cupcake, gluing together with frosting. Frost the cupcake. Place the blue sugar on a plate. Roll the sides of the cupcake in the blue sugar.

2. Frost eight regular-sized cupcakes. Dip the edges of the cupcakes in the sugar.

3. Place a candle and a Hanukkah candy or a dreidl in the center of each cupcake.

4. Arrange nine cupcakes on a tray in the shape of a menorah, with the shamus in the center.

MARDI GRAS CUPCAKES

No one knows for sure when Mardi Gras, meaning "Fat Tuesday," started, but many believe the roots lie in the Roman pagan holiday celebrating the beginning of spring. It evolved into a Catholic holiday and is tied to Lent and Easter. Also know as Carnival, it is celebrated around the world, but New Orleans is best known for this holiday in America.

The King Cake is a traditional Mardi Gras treat. The person who finds the hidden "baby" in his or her cupcake must provide the cupcakes next year.

You will need:
 Golden Cupcakes recipe (page 64)
 Vanilla Frosting recipe (page 92)
 One caramel square
 Purple, green, yellow, and orange food coloring
 Purple, green, and gold colored sugar
 Purple, green, and gold candy dots

1. Place the caramel square in one of the liners before baking. Bake and cool cupcakes.

2. Divide the frosting into three portions. With food coloring make one portion purple to represent justice, one green to represent faith, and one gold to represent power. Frost the cupcakes in a bull's-eye pattern.

3. Sprinkle cupcake tops with colored sugars.

4. Overlap the bull's-eye rings with matching candy dots.

PASSOVER CUPCAKES

In the days before Passover, Jews remove from the house and do not eat anything containing yeast. Today, yeast-free macaroons are a popular Passover dessert. Try these chocolate macaroon cupcakes for your celebration.

You will need:
Chocolate Macaroon Cupcakes recipe (page 59)
Chocolate Macaroon Glaze recipe (page 85)
Toasted coconut
Six-pointed star (or Star of David) candy
Chocolate chips

1. Bake, cool, and frost cupcakes. Sprinkle toasted coconut over the cupcake tops.
2. Place a six-pointed star candy in each center and upside down chocolate chips around the cupcake perimeters.

ST. PATRICK'S DAY CUPCAKES

People celebrate St. Patrick's Day with shamrocks, leprechauns, pots of gold, parades, wearing of the green, and drinking beer. I prefer Irish cream liqueur, so I have developed these cupcakes for the occasion. If you prefer beer, refer to the Chocolate Beer Cupcakes recipe (page 55).

You will need:
Irish Cream Cupcakes recipe (page 65)
Irish Cream Filling recipe (page 102)
Irish Cream Frosting recipe (page 87)
Fudge Frosting recipe (page 86)
Irish cream liqueur

Tiny Irish mugs
St. Patrick's Day stickers
Toothpicks

1. Bake and cool cupcakes. Remove two teaspoons of cake from the centers of the cupcakes with a grapefruit spoon. Save the removed cake. Fill the hole with filling. Replace the cake.

2. Frost the cupcakes with one frosting in the center and the other frosting around the perimeters .

3. Place a tiny mug on each cupcake top. Fill the mugs with Irish cream liqueur.

4. Place St. Patrick's Day stickers on the ends of toothpicks and stick them into the cupcakes.

chapter 7

Events and Occasions

BIRTHDAY CUPCAKES

Birthdays celebrate the guest of honor's uniqueness. Creating cupcakes that are themed with favorite hobbies, subjects, characters, and colors are perfect for a gathering at home or to share with the kids at school. For big kids or small these cupcakes will make the young at heart want to celebrate.

BIRTHDAY THEME CUPCAKES

You will need:

Birthday boy or girl's favorite cupcakes recipe
Birthday boy or girl's favorite frosting recipe
Colored sprinkles

Stickers, toys, and images in party theme
White glue
Toothpicks
Birthday candles

1. Bake, cool, and frost cupcakes. Decorate with colored sprinkles.

2. Using frosting as glue, attach theme toys and candies on the cupcake tops in playful patterns.

3. Attach stickers or glue images to toothpicks. Place candies on toothpick tops. Stick toothpicks into the cupcakes.

4. Place a birthday candle on each cupcake.

CANDLES CUPCAKES

You will need:
> *Birthday boy or girl's favorite cupcakes recipe*
> *Vanilla Frosting recipe (page 92)*
> *Food coloring*
> *Homemade molded candies (page 39)*
>
> *Candles*

1. Bake and cool cupcakes. Divide the frosting into two bowls. If desired, color the frosting the birthday child's favorite colors, frosting the cupcakes one color in the centers and the other color around the perimeters.

2. Place a candle for each year of age or a single candle into the cupcakes.

4. Place homemade candies in any remaining spaces.

HAPPY BIRTHDAY CUPCAKES

You will need:
> *Birthday boy or girl's favorite cupcakes recipe*
> *Favorite frosting recipe*
> *Royal Icing Recipe (page 91)*
> *Celebration Cookies recipe (page 95)*
> *Food coloring*
> *Nonpareils*
> *Candies, nuts, and snacks*
>
> *Alphabet cookie cutters*
> *Platter*
> *Pastry bag with writing tip*

On cake stand: Back row, left to right: Birthday Theme Cupcakes. Front row, left to right: Presents Cupcake, Polka-Dot Cupcake. On plates, left to right: Age Cookie Cupcake, Candles Cupcake.

Birthday Wish Cupcakes

No birthday celebration is complete without cupcakes, candles, and making a wish. Ever wonder what people wish for when they close their eyes? Birthday Wish Cupcakes are inspired by the most popular wishes: love, luck, peace, money, success, friendship. Think about what you wish for and create cupcakes that capture the theme. Or make a cupcake with a big question mark and keep people guessing.

You will need:

Favorite cupcakes recipe
Favorite frosting recipe
Royal Icing recipe (page 91)
Food coloring
Colored sugar
Candies (see step 3)

Candles
Pastry bag with writing tip

1. Bake your favorite cupcakes and prepare the Royal Icing. Divide the icing into three batches and color each a different color with food coloring. Frost the cupcakes one color in the

1. Prepare the Celebration Cookies batter. Make cookies that spell HAPPY BIRTHDAY and the name of the guest of honor. Bake and cool. Frost with icing and create patterns with a pastry bag.

2. Frost the cupcakes. Pour nonpareils in a small bowl. Dip the edges of the cupcakes in the nonpareils.

3. Place the cookies individually on the cupcakes to spell HAPPY BIRTHDAY and the name.

4. If there are remaining cupcakes, decorate with candy and nuts. Arrange in order on a platter. Place candy, nuts, and snacks on the platter around the cupcakes.

AGE COOKIE CUPCAKES

You will need:

Birthday boy's or girl's favorite cupcakes recipe
Vanilla Frosting recipe (page 92)
Celebration Cookies recipe (page 95)
Food coloring
Small candies
Colored sugar
Caramel candies
Nonpareils

Number cookie cutters
String licorice

1. Prepare the Celebration Cookies batter. Cut out the birthday boy or girl's age with numbered cookie cutters or a knife. Bake and cool.

2. Divide the frosting into two bowls. Color frosting in the birthday guest of honor's favorite colors. Frost the cupcakes with one color in the centers and the other around the perimeters. Sprinkle cupcakes with colored sugar.

3. Frost the cookies. Then attach small candies to the cookies.

4. Using frosting as glue, place number cookies in cupcake centers.

5. With a knife, frost the caramels and attach nonpareils or small candies to look like presents. Make a bow for each present out of string licorice. Place presents on the cupcake.

6. Place a candle on each cupcake.

center and another color around the perimeter.

2. Sprinkle cupcakes with colored sugar.

3. Place the third color frosting in a pastry bag.

- Peace cupcakes: Draw the lines of a peace sign

- Love cupcakes: Draw a heart and write the word LOVE on the cupcake. Attach candy hearts.

- Luck cupcakes: Create a four-leaf clover by making four hearts meet at a point in the center. Draw a stem.

- Friendship cupcakes: Place two round candies onto the cupcake to make two heads. Attach small candies or, with an edible marker, create happy faces. Write the word FRIENDSHIP.

- Money cupcakes: Draw a dollar sign. Top with candy coins.

- Success cupcakes: Place a large candy star on the cupcake with several smaller stars around it. Write the word SUCCESS.

4. Place a candle on each cupcake. Light it, close your eyes, and blow it out to make a wish.

POLKA-DOT CUPCAKES

You will need:

Birthday boy or girl's favorite cupcakes recipe
Vanilla Frosting recipe (page 92)
Food coloring
Colored sugars
Small circle candies
Medium circle candies
Large circle candies

Candles

1. Bake and cool cupcakes. Divide the frosting into small bowls and color with the guest of honor's favorite colors. Frost the cupcakes.

2. Sprinkle colored sugars over the cupcakes.

3. Using frosting as glue, make stacks of circle candies, some in two tiers and others in three tiers, to make polka-dots. Add them to cupcake tops..

PRESENTS CUPCAKES

You will need:

Birthday boy or girl's favorite cupcakes recipe, doubled
Vanilla Frosting recipe (page 92), doubled
Food coloring
Candies

Pastry bag with writing tip
8-inch or 9-inch cake pan
String licorice
Candle

1. Bake half of the cupcake batter in cupcake liners and the other half in a square cake pan; cool.

2. Cut the square cake into equal numbers of small and medium-sized squares. Cut the medium-sized squares slightly smaller than the diameter of the round cupcakes, and cut the small squares slightly smaller than the medium squares. Make as many squares of each size as you have cupcakes.

3. Make the frosting and divide it into three bowls. Color each batch the guest of honor's favorite colors with food coloring. Reserve some frosting for piping designs.

4. Frost the round cupcakes one color.

5. Place a medium-sized cake square on top of the round cupcake. Frost the square the second color. Decorate the sides with candies and piped frosting to make a pattern.

6. Place a small cake square on the top of the medium square. Frost the cake with the third color frosting.

7. Outline square presents with licorice ribbon and make a licorice bow on top.

8. Place a candle in the middle.

BABY CUPCAKES

New babies are excellent cause for merriment. Serve cupcakes at a baby shower, christening, or your next baby event. You can also bake them as a gift for the new parents and big bro and sis to celebrate the birth of the new arrival.

BABY CUPCAKES

You will need:

Favorite cupcakes recipe
Vanilla Frosting recipe (page 92)
Food coloring

Pastry bag with a large star-shaped tip
Mini baby bottles filled with candy or other baby decorations

1. Bake and cool cupcakes. Divide the frosting into two bowls, one large and one small, and color two different colors with food coloring. Frost the cupcakes with the color from the large bowl.

2. Place the second frosting color in a pastry bag and pipe a spiral around each cupcake top.

3. Top with mini baby bottles.

IT'S A BOY/IT'S A GIRL CUPCAKES

You will need:

Favorite cupcakes recipe
Vanilla Frosting recipe (page 92)
Food coloring
Candy balls

Baby doll toy
Lollipop with WELCOME, BABY banner

Pastry bag with a star tip

1. Divide the frosting into two bowls and color two different colors with food coloring. Frost the cupcakes with one color.

2. Place the second color of frosting in a pastry bag with a star tip. Decorate with a pattern around the edges.

3. Place candy balls around the inside perimeter of the trim.

4. Using frosting as glue, attach a baby doll in the center.

5. Add a store-bought lollipop with a baby announcement. To make your own, write "It's a girl" or "It's a boy" on sticker paper or card stock. Attach to a lollipop with tape or glue.

DAISY CUPCAKES

You will need:

Favorite cupcakes recipe
Vanilla Frosting recipe (page 92)
Colored sugar
Pink candy dots
Yellow candies
Candy hearts
Candy flowers (2 sizes)

Pastry bag with petal tip

1. Bake, cool, and frost cupcakes, reserving some frosting. Sprinkle colored sugar onto frosted cupcakes.

2. Place reserved frosting in a pastry bag. Make daisy shapes (see page 36).

3. Place a yellow candy in each flower center and pink candy dots around the petals.

4. Using frosting as glue, attach candy hearts around the cupcake perimeter.

5. Using frosting as glue, layer candy flowers on the candy hearts.

STAR CUPCAKES

You will need:
Favorite cupcakes recipe
Vanilla Frosting recipe (page 92)
Food coloring
Blue candy dots
Large, medium, and small candy stars

Ribbon with decorator's baby ornament
Pastry bag with large tip

1. Divide the frosting into two bowls and color two different colors with food coloring. Frost the cupcakes with one color.

2. Place the second color of frosting in a pastry bag. Make a star shape.

3. Place a large candy star in the center of the frosting star. Using frosting as glue, place a smaller one on top. Layer a smaller, different-colored star onto the larger ones.

4. Attach large candy stars around the cupcake.

5. Add blue candy dots in the remaining spaces.

6. Tie a ribbon with a decorator's baby ornament around the cupcake.

TWINS CUPCAKES

You will need:
Favorite cupcakes recipe
Vanilla Frosting recipe (page 92)
Food coloring
Colored sugar
Alphabet candy
Candy dots
Candy stars
Candy flowers

Ribbon with decorator's baby ornament

1. Bake and cool cupcakes. Divide the frosting into two bowls and tint with food coloring: perhaps pink and purple for twin girls, blue

Clockwise, from top: Baby Cupcake, It's a Boy, It's a Girl Cupcake, Welcome Baby Cupcake, Twins Cupcake, Star Cupcake, Daisy Cupcake

and green for twin boys, and blue and pink for boy-and-girl twins. Or pick more neutral colors.

2. Spread the frosting on the cupcakes to resemble yin-and-yang symbols.

3. Sprinkle each section with colored sugar that complements the frosting colors you've chosen.

4. As room allows, spell the twins' names on the cupcakes with alphabet candy.

5. Alternate candy dots and stars for boys, dots and flowers for girls, or both for a mixed set around the perimeters of the cupcakes.

WELCOME BABY CUPCAKES

You will need:
> *Favorite cupcakes recipe*
> *Vanilla Frosting recipe (page 92)*
> *Celebration Cookies recipe (page 95)*
> *Food coloring*
> *Colored sugar*
>
> *Round, flower, or star shaped cookie cutters*
> *Pastry bag with decorating and writing tips*
> *Decorator's plastic babies*

1. Bake round, star, or flower shaped Celebration Cookies. Cool.

2. Divide the frosting into two bowls and tint two different colors with food coloring. Reserve some frosting to use later. Frost the cupcakes with one color and the cookies with the other color.

3. Sprinkle colored sugar onto both cookies and cupcakes.

4. Place frosting in a pastry bag. Using a decorating tip, make a pattern around the perimeter of each cupcake. Write the baby's name on the cookies with frosting. Place the cookies in the cupcake centers. Place plastic babies onto the cookies.

WEDDING CUPCAKES

When it comes to putting a new twist on weddings, couples are always looking for unique ways to customize the event. That's why cupcakes have become a widely popular alternative to traditional wedding cakes. Based on tiered wedding cakes, these cupcakes are constructed from cupcakes made using three sizes of cupcake pans. Show them to your local baker for inspiration or make them yourself. They will also go over well at a wedding shower.

BRIDE AND GROOM CUPCAKES

You will need:
 Golden Cupcakes recipe (page 64)
 Chocolate Cupcakes recipe (page 58)
 Chocolate Frosting recipe (page 84)
 Raspberry Sauce recipe (page 100)
 Vanilla Frosting recipe (page 92)
 Candy flowers

 Bride-and-groom decorations
 Medium and large cupcake pans
 Card stock
 Ribbon and dried silk flowers
 White wine

1. Prepare the cupcake batters. These layered cupcake "towers" will each require one large and two medium cupcakes. To make medium and large Golden Cupcakes and Chocolate Cupcakes, pour the batters in both sizes of cupcake pans. Cool.

2. To make the bottom layers, frost the sides and perimeters of large cupcakes with Chocolate Frosting, then add a teaspoon of Raspberry Sauce in the center of the tops.

3. Flip medium cupcakes upside down onto the large cupcakes. Frost the sides with Vanilla Frosting. Spoon Raspberry Sauce on the tops.

4. Place another layer of medium cupcakes upside down on top of the cupcakes already stacked. Frost the sides of this top layer with Chocolate Frosting and the tops with Vanilla Frosting.

Old, New, Borrowed, Blue Cupcakes

*E*very bride needs something old, something new, something borrowed, something blue. Why shouldn't that something be tasty, too? Bring these cupcakes to a bridal shower, or feed them to the bride as a very lucky prewedding snack.

● ● ●

To begin, choose an old-time family favorite cupcake recipe (this will be the "old" part of the cupcake). For the "new" part of the cupcake, create a wonderful new design scheme for your cupcake, using the tiered cupcake diagrams and toppings schemes in Chapter 9 (see page 243). "Borrow" a white frosting recipe from a friend or family member on the bride's behalf. Color the frosting "blue" with food coloring. Enjoy!

5. Place a bride-and-groom cake decoration on each cupcake top.

6. Make an arch: Cut a ¼-inch strip of card stock paper long enough to arc over the cake decorations. Tape or glue 1-inch wire to each end. Cover it with candy flowers using glue. Curve the arch and stick the wire ends into the cupcake top.

7. Decorate the cupcakes with small candy hearts

8. Tie a ribbon with dried or silk flowers around the liner.

DIAMOND THREE-CITRUS CUPCAKES

You will need:
Lemon Cupcakes recipe (page 66)
Lime Icing recipe (page 87)
Orange Sauce recipe (page 100)
Candied Citrus Peel recipe (page 94)
White candy hearts
Diamond-shaped rock candies

Edible-ink pen
Mini, medium, and large cupcake pans

1. Prepare the cupcake batter. Divide the batter equally between mini, medium, and large cupcake pans. Bake and cool the cupcakes.

2. Make layered cupcakes: To make the bottom layer, frost the large cupcakes sides and perimeters with icing. Place a teaspoon of Orange Sauce on the tops.

3. Flip medium cupcakes upside down onto the large cupcakes. Frost the edges and the top perimeters with icing. Place a teaspoon of Orange Sauce in the middles.

4. Place mini cupcakes upside down on top. Frost the entire cupcake tower.

5. Place white heart and diamond shaped rock candies around the bases of the medium and mini cupcakes.

6. Write the names of the couple on two candy hearts with an edible ink pen. Place on the tops of the cupcakes.

7. Garnish with Candied Citrus Peel.

Clockwise, from top: Diamond Three-Citrus Cupcake, His and Her Family Cupcake, Bride and Groom Cupcake, Dove Cupcake, Tiered Almond Cupcake.

DOVE CUPCAKES

You will need:

Champagne Cupcakes recipe (page 53)
Champagne Buttercream Icing recipe (page 84)
Yellow food coloring
Strawberry Sauce recipe (page 101)
White sugar
White chocolate chips
White chocolate chunks

Mini and large cupcake pans
White wire
Plastic doves
Ribbon and dried or silk flowers

1. Prepare the cupcake batters. Bake the cupcakes in large and mini cupcake pans. These layered cupcakes will each require one large and two mini cupcakes. Cool.

2. Divide the icing into two bowls. Leave one batch white and make the other yellow with food coloring.

3. To make the bottom layers, frost the large cupcakes white around the sides and perimeters. Place a teaspoon of Strawberry Sauce in the center of each top.

4. Place mini cupcakes upside down on top of the large cupcakes. Frost the sides and perimeters yellow. Spread Strawberry Sauce on the tops.

5. Place another mini cupcake upside down on top. Frost white.

6. Sprinkle white sugar over the entire cupcake "tower."

7. Place white chocolate chips around the bases of the yellow cupcakes and white chocolate chunks on the tops.

8. Fasten white wire into two dove decorations. Attach doves to the sides of the mini cupcakes to look like they are flying.

9. Tie a ribbon with dried or silk flowers around the liner.

•*Note* This is a great conversation piece at an anniversary celebration as well. Display wedding, family photos, and current photos of the couple on anniversary cupcakes. For silver anniversary, use silver toppings, For golden anniversary, use gold toppings.

HIS AND HER FAMILY CUPCAKES

You will need:
  Favorite cupcakes recipe
  Vanilla frosting recipe (page 92)
  White sugar
  Silver candy balls

  Toothpicks
  Sticker paper, or paper and glue or tape
  Family wedding photographs or photocopies

  Large cupcake pan
  Medium cupcake pan
  Pastry bag with writing tip

1. Prepare the cupcake batter. Bake an equal number of medium cupcakes in greased cupcake pan and large cupcakes in liners.

2. Prepare the frosting. Divide the batch in half. Color one batch your favorite color and set aside. Frost the large cupcakes with the white frosting.

3. Set a medium-sized cupcake upside down on top of each large cupcake. Frost with remaining white frosting.

4. Sprinkle frosted cupcakes with white sugar.

5. Place colored frosting in pastry bag and pipe a design. (Sample templates: page 251). Add silver candy balls to the design.

6. Attach old wedding pictures and pictures of his and her family members to toothpicks with glue or tape. Place on the cupcakes.

TIERED ALMOND CUPCAKES

You will need:
  Almond Cupcakes recipe (page 49)
  Almond Frosting recipe (page 83)
  Whole plain or chocolate-covered almonds
  Sliced almonds
  Poppy seeds
  Chocolate leaves (page 38)
  Candied almonds

1. These layered cupcakes will each require two cupcakes. Bake the cupcakes in medium pans, half in cupcake liners and the other half in greased and floured pans. The lined cakes will be top layers. The unlined cakes will be bottom layers. Cool.

2. Frost the bottom layers. Place whole almonds or chocolate-covered almonds on cupcake tops.

3. Place the top-layer cupcakes upside down onto the frosted cupcakes. Frost the sides and tops.

4. Press sliced almonds into the sides of the cupcakes.

5. Place ½ teaspoon of poppy seeds in the center of the cupcake tops.

6. Place chocolate leaves on the top of each cupcake.

7. Place candied almonds in a flower shape on top of the leaves and around the poppy seeds.

TEEN TURNING POINTS CUPCAKES

Throughout the teen years, there are many milestones to celebrate. At your next party, serve these pretty, dreamy, glamorous, tasty cupcakes. Guests won't be able to get enough of what these are made of: sugar and spice and everything nice!

BAR/BAT MITZVAH CUPCAKES

You will need:
Favorite cupcakes recipe
Vanilla Frosting recipe (page 92)
Food coloring
Edible glitter or colored sugar

Square or rectangular cake pan
Large cupcake pan
Six-pointed star cookie cutter
Pastry bag with writing tip

1. Bake half of the batter in a cake pan, bake the other half in large cupcake pans. When cakes have cooled, cut the flat cake with a six-

pointed star cookie cutter that is slightly smaller than the cupcake tops. Make the same number of stars that you have cupcakes.

2. Divide the frosting into three bowls. Color your favorite colors with food coloring. Reserve some frosting for decorating.

3. Frost the cupcakes. Sprinkle edges with edible glitter or colored sugar.

4. Place the six-pointed star cake on top of large cupcakes. Frost the star with second color frosting.

5. Place the reserved frosting in a pastry bag. Outline the star with piping designs.

On cake stand, clockwise from top, left: Bar/Bat Mitzvah Cupcake, Graduation Cupcake, Sweet Sixteen Bow Cupcake. On tabletop, left to right: Crystal Flower Cupcake, Quinceañera Cupcake, Sugar and Spice and Everything Nice Cupcake.

Slumber Party

Having a slumber party? Buy some candy and make these cupcakes as entertainment at the party. Each person can make their own and customize them to their tastes. To create cupcakes as art objects, choose one or two cupcake recipes and play around with different candies using the circle templates and color palettes shown in chapter 9. Use the Mocha or Coffee Cupcakes recipes to stay awake extra late.

CRYSTAL FLOWER CUPCAKES

You will need:
Favorite cupcakes recipe
Royal Icing recipe (page 90)
Sugar Paste Icing recipe (page 92)
Crystal Edible Flowers recipe (page 96)
Food coloring
Colored sugar

Pastry bag with star tip
Circle cookie cutter

1. Color the Royal Icing with food coloring. Frost the cupcakes with this icing.

2. Divide the Sugar Paste Icing into two bowls. Color each batch a color that will match the Crystal Edible Flowers.

3. Make a basket weave with the Sugar Paste Icing (pages 41–42). Cut the basket weave with a circle cookie cutter slightly smaller than the cupcake. Place it on the cupcake.

4. Pipe the edges of the basket weave with Royal Icing.

5. Use frosting as glue to attach Crystal Edible Flowers to the cupcakes.

GRADUATION CUPCAKES

You will need:
Favorite cupcakes recipe
Vanilla Frosting recipe (page 92)
Food coloring
Chocolate Frosting recipe (page 84)
Black coloring gel
Square cookies
Black string licorice
Candy buttons

Mini and large cupcake pans
Pastry bag with small writing tip

1. Prepare the cupcake batter. Pour the batter into an equal number of mini and large cupcake pans. These cupcakes will each require one cupcake of each size. Bake and cool.

2. Prepare the Vanilla Frosting. Divide the frosting into two batches. Color each batch one of your school colors with food coloring. Reserve some frosting for writing. Frost the large cupcakes using the two school colors.

3. Prepare the Chocolate Frosting. Color the Chocolate Frosting black with coloring gel.

4. Flip mini cupcakes upside down on top of the large cupcakes. Using frosting as glue, place square cookies on top of the mini cupcakes. Frost the mini cupcakes and cookies black to make a cap.

5. Cut string licorice into small pieces. Group the pieces together to make a tassel. Place the tassel on top of the cap. Top off with a candy button.

6. Place colored frosting in a pastry bag. Write CLASS OF and the year or just the year on the cupcakes.

QUINCEAÑERA CUPCAKES

Hispanic girls all over the world celebrate a girl becoming a woman on her fifteenth birthday. Serve these tasty cupcakes, invite a friend's band to play live music, and dance all night.

You will need:
Almond Cupcakes recipe (page 49)
Marzipan recipe (page 99)
Red food coloring
Candy hearts

Rolling pin
Circle cookie cutter
Large heart cookie cutters
Number cookie cutters

1. Bake and cool cupcakes. Prepare the marzipan and divide into two batches, one large and one small. Tint the large batch pink and the small batch red with food coloring.

2. Roll out the pink marzipan with a rolling pin. Cut the icing with a circle cookie cutter a little smaller in diameter than the cupcakes. Place icing circles on the baked cupcakes.

3. With the heart cookie cutters emboss a large heart impression in the center of the cupcakes.

4. Roll out the red marzipan with a rolling pin. With number cookie cutters or a knife, cut out the number 15 as many times as you need to decorate all the cupcakes.

5. To make a rope border (page 41) roll the remaining red and pink marzipan into long thin strips. Twist the strips together to make a border around the cupcake perimeters.

6. Place candy hearts where the strips meet.

SUGAR AND SPICE AND EVERYTHING NICE CUPCAKES

You will need:
Spice Cupcakes recipe (page 77)
Sugar Paste Icing recipe (page 92)
Food coloring

Rolling pin
Assorted circle cookie cutters
Assorted flower cookie cutters

1. Prepare the Sugar Paste Icing. Divide it into two batches and color each a different color with food coloring. Reserve about one-third of a batch of each color. Place two other batches in a bowl and marbleize them, blending slightly with a knife.

2. Roll out the marbleized icing with a rolling pin. With a circle cookie cutter, cut the icing around the size of the diameter of the cupcakes. With a small cookie cutter emboss patterns in the circle. Place the Sugar Paste Icing circle on the cupcake.

3. Roll out the reserved colored Sugar Paste Icing. With flower cookie cutters, cut out icing. Then, with a different cookie cutter, emboss a pattern into the flower. Place on the center of the cupcake.

SWEET SIXTEEN BOW CUPCAKES

You will need:

Lemon Cupcakes recipe (page 66)
Royal Icing recipe (page 91)
Sugar Paste Icing recipe (page 92)
Food coloring

Rolling pin
Pastry bag with a decorator tip

1. Divide the icing into two batches and color them pastel colors with food coloring. Frost the cupcakes with one color.

2. Place the second color frosting into pastry bag and make a pattern around the edge of each cupcake.

3. Prepare the Sugar Paste Icing and prepare a Sugar Paste Bow (page 42). Place the bow in the center of each cupcake.

FUND-RAISER BAKE SALE CUPCAKES

Baking for a bake sale or fund-raiser is an enjoyable way to volunteer some of your time for an important cause. Cupcakes are definitely the best choice for a sale. They are a quick mass-produced confection that can be sold individually for a pretty good profit. These recipes and decorations are eye-catching and mouthwatering.

CANDY COIN CUPCAKES

You will need:

Chocolate Cupcakes recipe (page 58)
Chocolate Frosting recipe (page 84)
Chocolate sprinkles
White nonpareils
Candy coins

Sticker paper or paper and glue
Toothpicks

1. Bake, cool, and frost cupcakes. Pour chocolate sprinkles into a bowl. Dip the sides of the frosted cupcakes into the chocolate sprinkles.

2. Sprinkle white nonpareils in the center of the cupcake tops.

3. Make a flag: Write THANK YOU on sticker paper or regular paper. Wrap the stickers around or glue the signs to toothpicks. Push the flags into the cupcakes.

4. Place candy coins in the center of the cupcake tops.

THE COLOR OF MONEY CUPCAKES

You will need:
Lime Cupcakes recipe (page 66)
Lime Icing recipe (page 87)
Green food coloring
Green colored sugar
Green candies

Drinking straws
Glue or tape
Play money

1. Bake and cool cupcakes. Color the icing green with food coloring, and frost the cupcakes.

2. Sprinkle with green sugar. Attach green candies in patterns on the cupcakes.

3. Cut straws into 3-inch pieces. Glue or tape play money to straws. Place into cupcakes.

LUCKY CUPCAKES

You will need:
Golden Cupcakes recipe (page 64)
Vanilla Frosting recipe (page 92)
Large piece(s) of soft candy
Food coloring
Large candy dots
Colored sugar

Sticker paper or regular paper and glue
Toothpicks

1. Prepare cupcake batter and baking pans with liners. Hide a large piece of candy in the batter of one of the cupcakes. (If you would like several winners, place candies into several cupcakes.) Bake and cool.

Clockwise, from top, left: Raffle Cupcake, Organization Logo Cupcake, The Color of Money Cupcake, Candy Coin Cupcake, Thank-You Cupcake, Lucky Cupcake

2. Divide the frosting into two batches and tint them two different colors with food coloring. Frost cupcakes with one color for the center and the other color around the perimeter.

3. Place colored dots in a bowl. Dip the side of the cupcakes into dots.

4. Make question marks with candy dots on all of the cupcakes.

5. Make a sign that says LUCKY CUPCAKES on a piece of paper or sticker paper. Attach each sign to a toothpick and insert into each cupcake.

6. The person who purchases the cupcake with the candy in the middle is the winner. Treat him or her to a prize.

ORGANIZATION LOGO CUPCAKES

You will need:
Favorite cupcakes recipe
Favorite frosting recipe
Colored sugar
Candies

Organization logo
Photocopier or a scanner and printer
Toothpicks

1. Bake, cool, and frost cupcakes. Sprinkle frosted cupcakes with colored sugar.

2. Place candies around the cupcake perimeters.

3. To make a pennant flag: With permission, photocopy your organization's logo onto regular paper or sticker paper, about 2 inches tall. You can also scan the logo into a computer and print it out. Cut out the logo in a triangle and attach it to a toothpick with tape or glue. Push the toothpick into the cupcake.

RAFFLE CUPCAKES

You will need:
Favorite cupcakes recipe
Vanilla Frosting recipe (page 92)
Food coloring
Colored sprinkles

Pastry bag with writing tip
Raffle tickets
Glue
Toothpicks

1. Bake and cool cupcakes. Divide the frosting into two bowls, one large and one small. The large bowl will be used for frosting the cupcakes, and the small bowl for piping. Tint frosting with food coloring to match the colors of your event or organization.

2. Place colored sprinkles in a bowl. Dip the sides of the cupcakes in the sprinkles.

3. Fill the pastry bag with the frosting from the small bowl. Write the name of the event or the organization on the cupcakes.

4. Reserve raffle numbers in a bowl. Glue raffle tickets to toothpicks. Place on cupcake tops.

5. Pull a winning ticket from the bowl and treat the winner to a prize. You can have several winners if you like.

THANK-YOU CUPCAKES

You will need:
Favorite cupcakes recipe
Favorite frosting recipe
Colored nonpareils
Alphabet candy
Candy hearts

1. Bake, cool, and frost cupcakes. Pour colored nonpareils into a bowl.

2. With alphabet candy write THANK YOU on the cupcakes.

3. Place candy hearts around the word YOU.

Kids' Cupcakes

LEMONADE STAND CUPCAKES

Stand out from the competition—sell stylish lemon cupcakes in addition to lemonade at your sidewalk stand. These cupcakes are guaranteed to create a summer afternoon of fun. Price them individually or by the dozen. Remember, time is money so keep your designs simple.

LEMON COCONUT CUPCAKES

You will need:
> *Lemon Cupcakes recipe (page 66)*
> *Lemon Icing recipe (page 87)*
> *Yellow nonpareils*
> *Shredded coconut*
> *Lemon ball candy*

1. Ice the cupcakes, reserving a few tablespoons of icing to use as glue.
2. Pour the nonpareils in a small bowl. Dip the edges of the cupcakes in the nonpareils.
3. Sprinkle the shredded coconut onto each cupcake.

On cake stand, clockwise from top, left: Lemon Meringue Cupcake, Lemon Lime Cupcake, Lemon Polka-Dot Cupcake, Lemon Coconut Cupcake; Center: Lemon Orange Cupcake. On tabletop: Totally Lemon Cupcake.

4. Dip the bottoms of lemon ball candies into the icing. Place a few candies on each cupcake.

LEMON LIME CUPCAKES

You will need:
> *Lemon Cupcakes recipe (page 66)*
> *Lemon Icing recipe (page 87)*
> *Yellow food coloring*
> *Green sugar*
> *Yellow nonpareils*
> *Lime candies*

1. Color the icing yellow with a few drops of food coloring. Ice the cupcakes.

2. Pour the nonpareils in a small bowl. Dip the edges of the cupcakes in the nonpareils.

3. Sprinkle green sugar in the center of each cupcake.

4. Place lime candies on each cupcake.

LEMON MERINGUE CUPCAKES

You will need:
> *Lemon Cupcakes recipe (page 66)*
> *Lemon Icing recipe (page 87)*
> *Yellow food coloring*
> *White and yellow nonpareils*
> *Store-bought meringue cookies*

1. Color the icing yellow with a few drops of food coloring. Ice the cupcakes.

2. Mix the white and yellow nonpareils in a small bowl. Dip the edges of the cupcakes in the nonpareils.

3. Place one meringue cookie on the top of each cupcake.

Lemonade Stand Tips

First, bake at least two batches of cupcakes and mix up some great lemonade. Here's a recipe you can try:

LEMONADE

8 lemons
1 cup sugar
2 trays ice cubes
3 ½ quarts water

Roll the lemons to help release their juices. Then squeeze the lemons on a juicer into a bowl. Remove the pits. Transfer the lemon juice into a pitcher and add remaining ingredients. Stir until sugar is dissolved.

Now, follow these easy steps and get ready to open up shop.

1. Location is everything. An actively used street corner is the best place to set up your stand. Decorate your table with a colorful tablecloth, banners, and poster-board signs. To look like a true professional, arrange your cupcakes on cake stands and fancy plates.

2. To advertise, make signs and hang them around the neighborhood. Don't forget to play up the uniqueness of your stand: Lemon Cupcakes for Sale!

3. To decide on the price of your cupcakes, add up the costs of preparing them and divide by the number of cupcakes you have. Mark them up as much as you like, making the unit price at least double your ingredients costs to pay for your time and other expenses. Use the same rule for the lemonade. To encourage buyers to purchase six cupcakes or a full dozen, give a slight discount for quantity. Don't forget to bring small change for big bills.

4. Call friends and family members and invite them to your sale: They make the best customers and assistants. If they help out, reward them with free cupcakes or part of the profits.

Good luck!

LEMON ORANGE CUPCAKES

You will need:

Lemon Cupcakes recipe (page 66)
Lemon Icing recipe (page 87)
Yellow food coloring
Orange nonpareils
Lemon and orange wedge candies

1. Color the icing yellow with a few drops of food coloring. Ice the cupcakes.

2. Pour the nonpareils in a small bowl. Dip the edges of the cupcakes in the nonpareils.

3. Before the icing hardens, sprinkle the cupcakes with orange sprinkles.

4. Place lemon and orange wedge candies on each cupcake.

LEMON POLKA-DOT CUPCAKES

You will need:

Lemon Cupcakes recipe (page 66)
Lemon Icing recipe (page 87)
Yellow food coloring
Yellow nonpareils
White chocolate chips

1. Color the icing yellow with a few drops of food coloring. Ice the cupcakes.

2. Pour the nonpareils in a small bowl. Dip the cupcakes in the nonpareils.

3. Place several white chocolate chips upside down and evenly spaced on cupcakes to make polka dots.

TOTALLY LEMON CUPCAKES

You will need:

Lemon Cupcakes recipe (page 66)
Lemon Icing recipe (page 87)

Yellow food coloring
Yellow colored sugar
Lemon candy
Yellow nonpareils
Yellow dots

1. Color the icing yellow with a few drops of food coloring. Ice the cupcakes.

2. Pour the nonpareils in a small bowl. Dip the edges of the cupcakes in the nonpareils.

3. Sprinkle the cupcakes with yellow colored sugar.

4. Place yellow dots around the edges and a lemon candy in the center of each cupcake.

FAVORITE FOODS CUPCAKES

CHOCOLATE PRETZELS CUPCAKES

You will need:
Chocolate Cupcakes recipe (page 58)
Vanilla Frosting recipe (page 92)
Chocolate-covered pretzels (page 39)
Candy dots
Chocolate chips

1. Bake, cool, and frost cupcakes. Place a chocolate-covered pretzel in the center of each frosted cupcake top.

2. Alternate candy dots and chocolate chips in a circle around cupcake perimeters.

GUMBALL AND GUMMY BEAR CUPCAKES

You will need:
Golden Cupcakes recipe (page 64)
Vanilla Frosting recipe (page 92)
Candy crystals

Gummy bears
Gumballs

Toothpicks

1. Bake, cool, and frost cupcakes. Sprinkle candy crystals on the tops of frosted cupcakes.

2. Place gummy bears around the perimeters.

3. With the tip of a knife make a tiny hole in the gumballs. Insert toothpicks into the holes. Stick the toothpicks into the cupcakes.

HOT CHOCOLATE CUPCAKES

You will need:
Chocolate Cupcakes recipe (page 58)
Marshmallow Frosting recipe (page 89)
Store-bought whipped topping
Cocoa powder
Mini marshmallows

1. Bake, cool, and frost cupcakes. Spoon a tablespoon or two of whipped topping over frosted cupcakes.

2. Sprinkle cupcakes with cocoa powder.

3. Top the cupcakes with mini marshmallows.

PEANUT BRITTLE AND JELLY CUPCAKES

You will need:

Peanut Butter Cupcakes recipe (page 71)

Cream Cheese frosting (page 86)

Fruit jam (strawberry, raspberry, grape)

Peanuts

Peanut brittle

1. Frost the cupcakes. With a knife, spread your favorite fruit jam on the top of the frosted cupcakes. They will be sticky.

2. Sprinkle peanuts on the jam. Stick a slice of peanut brittle into the cupcake.

PEANUT BUTTER CHOCOLATE CHIP CUPCAKES

You will need:

Peanut Butter Cupcakes recipe (page 71)

Chocolate Frosting recipe (page 84)

2 cups chocolate chips, plus some for decorating

Chocolate sprinkles

Mini peanut butter cups

Candy-coated peanuts

1. Add 2 cups of chocolate chips to cupcake batter. Mix well. Bake and cool.

2. Frost the cupcakes, reserving some frosting to use as glue.

3. Pour chocolate sprinkles into a small bowl. Dip the perimeters of the cupcakes into the chocolate sprinkles.

4. Place an unwrapped mini peanut butter cup in the center of each cupcake top. Frost the top of each peanut butter cup so they appear to be frosted cupcakes. Put a chocolate chip on top

5. Place candy-coated peanuts and chocolate chips alternately around each cupcake's perimeter.

Clockwise, from left: Chocolate Pretzel Cupcake, Peanut Butter Chocolate Chip Cupcake, Gumball and Gummy Bear Cupcake, Peanut Brittle and Jelly Cupcake, S'mores Cupcake, Hot Chocolate Cupcake.

S'MORES CUPCAKES

You will need:
> Chocolate Chocolate Chip Cupcakes recipe (page 58)
> Marshmallow Frosting recipe (page 89)
> Large marshmallows
> Graham crackers or chocolate-covered graham crackers
> Chocolate fudge

1. Pour cupcake batter into liners until about half full. Submerge a marshmallow into each cup. Bake and cool.

2. Prepare the frosting. Frost the cupcakes, reserving some frosting to use for s'mores.

3. To build a s'more on top: Spread chocolate fudge, marshmallow frosting, and whole marshmallows between two graham crackers. Place one s'more on the top of each cupcake.

FRIENDLY FACES CUPCAKES

Freshly frosted cupcakes make fantastic canvases on which to create friendly, silly expressions. Use ordinary store-bought candies to craft these gregarious characters. There are even templates for additional face designs in the Design Elements chapter (see page 251).

CONE NOSE CUPCAKES

You will need:
> Favorite cupcakes recipe
> Favorite frosting recipe
> Sugar cones
> Candy almonds
> Candy flowers
> Mint chips
> Colored shredded coconut

1. Bake, cool, and frost cupcakes. Break the tips off sugar cones about 2 inches from the end to make noses. Place one in the center of each frosted cupcake.

2. Place two candy almonds on the cupcakes to make eyes. Using frosting as glue, attach candy flowers on top of the almonds.

3. Place mint chips upside down in a semicircle to form a mouth.

4. Sprinkle colored shredded coconut on top to make hair.

Clockwise, from top: Gummy Hair Cupcake, Cookie Face Cupcake, Star Hair Cupcake, Cone Nose Cupcake, Peeking Face Cupcake, Crispy Face Cupcake.

COOKIE FACE CUPCAKES

You will need:

Favorite cupcakes recipe
Favorite frosting recipe
Rainbow nonpareils
Shaped cookies
Mint chips
Candy hearts
Large candy circles

1. Bake, cool, and frost cupcakes.

2. Pour rainbow nonpareils into a small bowl. Dip the frosted cupcakes into the nonpareils.

3. Spread frosting on the bottom and top of each shaped cookie. Place cookie on each cupcake.

4. Attach two large candy circles to the cookie to make eyes. Using frosting as glue, attach a mint chip to each eye. Add a candy heart mouth.

CRISPY FACE CUPCAKES

You will need:

Favorite cupcakes recipe
Favorite frosting recipe
Rice Cereal Topping recipe (page 100)
Nuts
String licorice
Chocolate imperial candies
Star candies

1. Bake, cool, and frost cupcakes.

2. Shape the Rice Cereal Topping into 1½ inch balls. Spread frosting on the bottom and top of each ball. Attach one to the center of each frosted cupcake.

3. Cut a small piece of string licorice. Dip one side in frosting and place a smile on the rice ball.

4. With frosting, glue on two chocolate imperial candies as eyes and a star candy as a nose.

5. Place nuts around the crispy face.

GUMMY HAIR CUPCAKES

You will need:
Favorite cupcakes recipe
Favorite frosting recipe
Gummy worms
Assorted round candies
Banana candies
Candy dots

1. Bake, cool, and frost cupcakes. Attach gummy worms to the frosted cupcakes to make long hair.

2. Using frosting as glue, stack round candies to make eyes. Add a round candy for nose. Attach a banana candy to make the mouth.

3. Sprinkle on candy dots as freckles.

PEEKING FACE CUPCAKES

Favorite cupcakes recipe
Favorite frosting recipe
Candy dots
Candy slices
Banana-shaped candies
Cinnamon imperials

1. Bake, cool, and frost cupcakes. Place candy dots around the perimeter of the frosted cupcakes.

2. Place a candy slice in the middle of each cupcake.

3. Break banana-shaped candies in half. Dip broken ends into the frosting. Place a candy half on the candy slice to make noses and horns.

4. With frosting, glue two cinnamon imperial candies on candy slices to make eyes.

STAR HAIR CUPCAKES

You will need:

Favorite cupcakes recipe
Favorite frosting recipe
Gummy stars
Crescent-shaped gummy candies
Cinnamon imperials
Round gummy candy
Candy crystals

1. Bake, cool, and frost cupcakes. Place gummy stars halfway around the perimeter of frosted cupcakes to make hair.

2. Place crescent-shaped gummy candies on the cupcake tops to make eyes. Using frosting as glue, attach cinnamon imperials to the eyes.

3. Place a round gummy candy in the center of the cupcake tops to make noses.

4. Use crescent-shaped gummy candies to make mouths.

5. Sprinkle on candy crystals as freckles.

KIDS' WORLD CUPCAKES

Turn your favorite small toys into cool cupcake decorations. Party stores, craft stores, superstores, supermarkets, cake decorating stores, candy stores, and toy stores are filled with a huge selection of objects that can be used to decorate cupcakes. You may not find exactly the same toppings you see here but you will definitely find wonderful inspiration for creation. Go crazy! These cupcakes are as much fun to play with as they are to eat!

CAR CUPCAKES

You will need:

Favorite cupcakes recipe
Chocolate Frosting recipe (page 84)

Chopped nuts
Sugar cones

Toy cars

1. Bake, cool, and frost cupcakes. Pour the nuts into a small bowl. Dip the frosted cupcakes into the nuts to make rocks.

2. Using frosting as glue, attach a toy car to each cupcake.

3. Break a sugar cone into pieces, leaving jagged edges. Stick the cone pieces into the cupcakes to look like large rocks.

CONSTRUCTION CUPCAKES

You will need:
Favorite cupcakes recipe
Chocolate Frosting recipe (page 84)
Granola
Chocolate-covered raisins
Graham crackers, crushed
Marshmallows

Construction toys

1. Bake, cool, and frost cupcakes. Place granola in a small bowl. Dip the frosted cupcakes into granola to make gravel.

2. With the frosting, glue a construction toy onto each cupcake. Place chocolate-covered raisins around the toy to look like rocks.

3. Crush graham crackers in a small bowl. Cover a marshmallow with frosting. Dip the marshmallow into the crumbs. Using frosting as glue, attach the "boulder" to the construction toy.

MOON WALKER CUPCAKES

You will need:
Favorite cupcakes recipe
Vanilla Frosting recipe (page 92)
Mini marshmallows

Space vehicle toys

1. Bake and cool cupcakes. Reserve some frosting to use as glue. Frost the cupcakes white to look like the moon. Top with marshmallows.

2. Attach a space vehicle toy on the marshmallows with frosting.

3. Top with a flag.

DINOSAUR CUPCAKES

You will need:

Favorite cupcakes recipe

Chocolate Frosting recipe (page 84)

Large rock candies

Chopped nuts

Dinosaur toys

Back row, left to right: Construction Cupcake, Pirate Treasure Cupcake. Middle row, left to right: Moon Walker Cupcake, Skateboard Cupcake, Butterfly Cupcake, Car Cupcake. Front row, left to right: Dinosaur Cupcake, Ring Cupcake.

1. Bake, cool, and frost cupcakes. Place a dinosaur toy on each frosted cupcake top.

2. Surround the dinosaur with large rock candies.

3. Place chopped nuts in remaining spaces to look like small rocks.

PIRATE TREASURE CUPCAKES

You will need:
> *Favorite cupcakes recipe*
> *Vanilla Frosting recipe (page 92)*
> *Food coloring*
> *Colored sugar*
> *Sprinkles*
> *Jelly beans*
> *Candy coins*
>
> *Toy pirates*

1. Bake and cool cupcakes. Color the frosting your favorite color with food coloring. Frost the cupcakes, reserving some frosting to use as glue.

2. Scatter colored sugar and sprinkles over the cupcakes until surface is covered.

3. Using frosting as glue, attach a toy pirate to each cupcake.

4. Place jelly beans and candy coins on the cupcakes to look like treasures.

RING CUPCAKES

You will need:
> *Favorite cupcakes recipe*
> *Favorite frosting recipe*
> *Food coloring*
> *Candy crystals*
> *Candy rings*
> *Rock candies*

1. Bake and cool cupcakes. Color the frosting your favorite color with food coloring. Frost the cupcakes.

2. Pour candy crystals into a small bowl. Dip the frosted cupcakes into the crystals.

3. Place candy rings and rock candies on top.

BUTTERFLY CUPCAKES

You will need:

> *Favorite cupcakes recipe*
> *Favorite frosting recipe*
> *Food coloring*
> *Small candy flowers*
>
> *Toy butterflies*
> *Toothpicks*

1. Bake and cool cupcakes. Color the frosting your favorite color with food coloring. Frost the cupcakes.

2. Cover frosted cupcakes with small candy flowers.

3. Place toy butterflies on cupcake tops. Place toothpicks as supports when necessary.

SKATEBOARD CUPCAKES

You will need:

> *Favorite cupcakes recipe*
> *Vanilla Frosting recipe (page 92)*
> *Food coloring*
> *Colored sprinkles*
> *Large candies*
>
> *Toy skateboards*

1. Bake and cool cupcakes. Color the frosting your favorite color with food coloring. Frost the cupcakes, reserving some frosting to use as glue.

2. Scatter sprinkles on the frosted cupcakes.

3. Place large candies on the cupcakes. They will be used to tilt the skateboards at an angle.

4. Using frosting as glue, attach the skateboard to each cupcakes.

TOY ANIMALS CUPCAKES

Creating these toy animal cupcakes is as much fun as a day at the zoo. Moo! Oink!

ALLIGATOR CUPCAKES

You will need:
Favorite cupcakes recipe
Vanilla Frosting recipe (page 92)
Brown and green food coloring
Green and brown licorice

Toy alligators

1. Bake and cool cupcakes. Divide the frosting into two small bowls. Color one batch of frosting brown and the other green with food coloring. Reserve some frosting to use as glue.

2. Place a large amount of both frostings on the cupcakes. Swirl them together to look like a swamp.

3. Attach toy alligators to the cupcakes.

4. Cut green and brown licorice into small pieces to look like swamp grass. Surround the alligators with licorice pieces.

COW CUPCAKES

You will need:
Favorite cupcakes recipe
Vanilla Frosting recipe (page 92)
Green food coloring
Green shredded coconut
Green licorice

Toy cows

1. Bake and cool cupcakes. Color the frosting green with food coloring. Frost the cupcakes.

2. Pour the green coconut into a bowl. Dip the cupcakes into the coconut.

3. Cut green licorice into spiky pieces 1–2 inches long. Stick them into the cupcakes.

4. Using frosting as glue, attach toy cows to the cupcake tops. Place them so they look like the cows are eating the grass.

FLAMINGO CUPCAKES

You will need:
Favorite cupcakes recipes
Favorite frosting recipes
Green food coloring
Green shredded coconut
Tiny candy flowers

Pink flamingo drink stirrers

1. Bake and cool cupcakes. Color the frosting green with food coloring. Frost the cupcakes.

2. Pour the green coconut into a bowl. Dip the frosted cupcakes into the coconut.

3. Using frosting as glue, attach candy flowers to the coconut.

4. Stick pink flamingo drink stirrers into each cupcake.

HORSE CUPCAKES

You will need:
Favorite cupcakes recipe
Chocolate Frosting recipe (page 84)
Granola
Graham crackers, crushed
Large marshmallows

Toy horses

1. Bake, cool, and frost cupcakes. Place granola into a small bowl. Dip the frosted cupcakes into the granola.

2. Place crushed graham crackers into a small bowl. Cover marshmallows with frosting. Dip the marshmallows into graham cracker crumbs. Using frosting as glue, attach marshmallows to the cupcakes to make mountains.

3. Using frosting as glue, attach toy horses to the cupcakes.

Back row, left to right: Flamingo Cupcake, Peacock Cupcake. Middle row, left to right: Horse Cupcake, Penguin Cupcake, Cow Cupcake. Front row, left to right: Alligator Cupcake, Pig Pen Cupcake, Turtle Cupcake.

PEACOCK CUPCAKES

Favorite cupcakes recipe
Favorite frosting recipe
Food coloring
Candy pebbles

Paper peacocks

1. Bake and cool cupcakes. Color the frosting your favorite color with food coloring. Frost the cupcakes.
2. Sprinkle candy pebbles over the cupcakes.
3. Place paper peacock in the center of each cupcake top.

PENGUIN CUPCAKES

You will need:
Favorite cupcakes recipe
Vanilla Frosting recipe (page 92)
Flaked coconut
Mini and large marshmallows
Mini and large chocolate imperials

Toy penguins

1. Bake, cool, and frost cupcakes. Pour the coconut into a small bowl. Dip the frosted cupcakes into the coconut.
2. Using frosting as glue, attach toy penguins to the cupcake tops.
3. Attach the marshmallows to the cupcakes.
4. Glue chocolate imperials to the marshmallows.

PIG PEN CUPCAKES

You will need:
Favorite cupcakes recipe
Chocolate Frosting recipe (page 84)

Graham crackers
Chocolate-covered raisins

Toy pigs

1. Bake, cool, and frost cupcakes. Crush graham crackers in a small bowl. Dip frosted cupcakes into the crumbs. With a knife, arrange the crumbs to look like the mud.

2. Using frosting as glue, attach chocolate-covered raisins to look like rocks.

3. Attach toy pigs to the cupcake. Spread some frosting on them to make the pigs look messy.

TURTLE CUPCAKES

You will need:
Favorite cupcakes recipe
Vanilla Frosting recipe (page 92)
Orange and blue food coloring
Graham crackers, crushed

Toy turtles
Small candy rocks

1. Bake and cool cupcakes. Divide the frosting into three small bowls. Keep one bowl of frosting white and color the others blue and orange with food coloring.

2. Spread orange frosting on one quarter of each cupcake top.

3. Place a large amount of blue and white frostings on the other three quarters of the cupcake. Swirl the frostings together to look like water.

4. Sprinkle graham cracker crumbs on the orange frosting to resemble sand.

5. Bury toy turtles partway in the blue frosting to look like they are emerging from the water.

6. Place candy rocks on the beach.

Become a Cupcake Designer

Cupcakes are more than mini versions of cakes—they are design objects. Like fashion, there is a look for every occasion, a style for each individual. Cupcakes are like interior decorating. Adding a few elements and changing a few details sets a new stage. Rethink cupcakes.

To become a cupcake designer:

- Start a scrapbook of inspirational images and patterns you enjoy.

- Set up a toolbox filled with cookie cutters, pastry bags and decorator's tips, food colorings, spreading knives, and inedible decorations.

- Ingredients are the cupcake designer's palette. Sugars, toppings, and candies come in many colors, tastes, textures, shapes, and sizes. Purchase an assortment of interesting toppings that you can create with.

- Refer to your own inspirational images and palettes to create cupcakes that are uniquely your own!

chapter 9

Flavor Combinations and Design Elements

Cupcakes and Frosting Suggestions

Do you have a fondness for experimenting with different taste combinations? While chocolate and vanilla frosting taste great, for most cupcakes recipes there are many other cupcake, frosting, and topping variations to explore. This chart partners all-time favorites and some classics.

● ● ●

ALMOND CUPCAKES   Almond Frosting
Coffee Cream Cheese Frosting
Dark Chocolate Icing
Liqueur Icing
Marzipan
White Chocolate Buttercream
Frosting

APPLE CUPCAKES	Caramel Topping
	Ginger Cream Cheese Frosting
	Maple Cream Cheese Frosting
	Peanut Butter Frosting
	Walnut Apple Raisin Topping
BANANA CUPCAKES	Banana Coconut Frosting
	Chocolate Macaroon Glaze
	Fudge Frosting
	Toasted Coconut Cream Cheese Frosting
	White Chocolate Buttercream Frosting
BITTERSWEET MOLTEN CHOCOLATE CUPCAKES	Marshmallow Frosting
	Raspberry or Strawberry Sauce
	Vanilla or Chocolate Ice Cream
	Whipped Cream
	White or Dark Chocolate Sauce
BLACK BOTTOM CUPCAKES	Cream Cheese Frosting
	Irish Cream Frosting
	Maple Cream Cheese Frosting
	Raspberry or Strawberry Sauce
	Strawberry Frosting
	White or Dark Chocolate Sauce
	White or Dark Chocolate Gnache
BLUEBERRY CUPCAKES	Cream Cheese Frosting
	Coconut Pecan Frosting
	Ginger Cream Cheese Frosting
	Lemon Icing
	Vanilla Frosting
BLUEBERRY RASPBERRY CUPCAKES	Chocolate Frosting
	Cream Cheese Frosting
	Maple Cream Cheese Frosting

Raspberry Sauce
White Chocolate Buttercream Frosting

BROWNIE CUPCAKES

Banana Coconut Frosting
Chocolate Ganache
Dark Chocolate Icing
Licorice Frosting

CARAMEL APPLE
CUPCAKES

Browned Butter Icing
Caramel Topping
Ginger Cream Cheese Frosting
Maple Cream Cheese Frosting
Rum Syrup

CHAMPAGNE
CUPCAKES

Almond Frosting
Champagne Buttercream Icing
Chocolate Ganache
Strawberry Sauce
Toasted Coconut Cream Cheese
  Frosting
White Chocolate Buttercream Frosting

CHEESECAKE
CUPCAKES

Strawberry, Raspberry, or
  Orange Sauce
White or Dark Chocolate Ganache
White or Dark Chocolate Sauce

CHERRY CORDIAL
CUPCAKES

Dark Chocolate Icing
Fudge Frosting
Liqueur Icing
Rum Syrup
White Chocolate Buttercream Frosting

CHOCOLATE BEER
CUPCAKESS

Banana Coconut Frosting
Chocolate Frosting
Fudge Frosting

CHOCOLATE BEER CUPCAKES (continued)	Maple Cream Cheese Frosting
	Spiked Orange Frosting
	White Chocolate Buttercream Frosting
CHOCOLATE CARROT CUPCAKES	Chocolate Cream Cheese Frosting
	Cream Cheese Frosting
	Ginger Cream Cheese Frosting
	Maple Cream Cheese Frosting
	Spiked Orange Frosting
	Toasted Coconut Cream Cheese
CHOCOLATE CHIP CINNAMON CUPCAKES	Cinnamon Whipped Cream
	Fudge Frosting
	Ginger Cream Cheese Frosting
	Maple Cream Cheese Frosting
	Vanilla Frosting
	White Chocolate Buttercream Frosting
CHOCOLATE CHOCOLATE CHIP COOKIE CUPCAKES	Hot Fudge and Whipped Cream
	Peppermint Cream Cheese Frosting
	Rich Chocolate Frosting
	Rosewater Icing
	Strawberry Frosting
CHOCOLATE CUPCAKES*	Liqueur Icing
	Marshmallow Frosting
	Peanut Butter Frosting
	Spiked Orange Frosting
	Strawberry, Orange, or Raspberry Sauce
	White or Dark Chocolate Ganache
CHOCOLATE MACAROON CUPCAKES	Banana Coconut Frosting
	Chocolate Macaroon Glaze

Almost every frosting and icing partners well with this recipe. Try some listed here.

	Coconut Pecan Frosting
	Cream Cheese Frosting
	Dark Chocolate Icing
	Toasted Coconut Cream Cheese Frosting
CHOCOLATE RASPBERRY CUPCAKES	Cream Cheese Frosting
	Dark Chocolate Icing
	Marshmallow Frosting
	Raspberry Sauce
	White Chocolate Buttercream Frosting
COFFEE CUPCAKES	Chocolate Frosting
	Coffee Cream Cheese Frosting
	Irish Cream Frosting
	Licorice Frosting
	Mocha Frosting
	Mocha Sauce
COOKIES AND CREAM CUPCAKES	Fudge Frosting
	Marshmallow Frosting
	Mocha Frosting
CORN CUPCAKES	Browned Butter Icing
	Chocolate Frosting
	Coconut Pecan Frosting
	Cream Cheese Frosting
	Ginger Cream Cheese Frosting
	Peanut Butter Frosting
CRANBERRY CUPCAKES	Dark Chocolate Icing
	Ginger Cream Cheese Frosting
	Maple Cream Cheese Frosting
	Toasted Coconut Cream Cheese Frosting

CREAM-FILLED CUPCAKES	Dark Chocolate Icing
	Irish Cream Filling
	Pastry Cream
	Tiramisù Cream
	White Chocolate Buttercream Frosting
	White or Dark Chocolate Ganache
EGGNOG CUPCAKES	Cinnamon Whipped Cream
	Liqueur Icing
	Rich Chocolate Frosting
	Rum Syrup
	White Chocolate Buttercream Frosting
GERMAN CHOCOLATE CUPCAKES	Banana Coconut Frosting
	Chocolate Frosting
	Coconut Pecan Frosting
	Rich Chocolate Frosting
	Toasted Coconut Cream Cheese Frosting
	White Chocolate Buttercream Frosting
GINGERBREAD CUPCAKES	Banana Coconut Frosting
	Cream Cheese Frosting
	Ginger Cream Cheese Frosting
	Lemon Icing
	Maple Cream Cheese Frosting
GOLDEN CUPCAKES*	Raspberry, Strawberry, or Orange Sauce
	Royal Icing
	Strawberry Frosting
	White or Dark Chocolate Ganache
HAZELNUT COFFEE CUPCAKES	Coffee Cream Cheese Frosting
	Fudge Frosting

*Almost every frosting and icing partners well with this recipe. Try some listed here.

Irish Cream Frosting
Mocha Frosting
Mocha Sauce
Rich Chocolate Frosting

IRISH CREAM CUPCAKES
Coffee Cream Cheese Frosting
Fudge Frosting
Irish Cream Frosting
Mocha Frosting
Mocha Sauce
Rich Chocolate Frosting

JAVA CHIP CUPCAKES
Coffee Cream Cheese Frosting
Dark Chocolate Icing
Irish Cream Frosting
Mocha Frosting
Mocha Sauce
Peppermint Cream Cheese Frosting

KAHLÚA CUPCAKES
Coffee Cream Cheese Frosting
Dark Chocolate Icing
Mocha Frosting
Mocha Sauce
Tiramisù Cream
White Chocolate Buttercream Frosting

LEMON CUPCAKES
Lemon Icing
Strawberry Frosting
Toasted Coconut Cream Cheese
    Frosting

LEMON GINGER POPPY SEED CUPCAKES
Ginger Frosting
Lemon Icing
Orange Sauce
White Chocolate Buttercream Frosting

LICORICE CUPCAKES	Licorice Frosting
	Marshmallow Frosting
	Peppermint Cream Cheese Frosting
	Vanilla Frosting
	White Chocolate Buttercream Frosting
LIME CUPCAKES	Lemon Icing
	Lime Icing
	Rum Syrup
	Spiked Orange Frosting
LOW-FAT CARROT CUPCAKES	Low-Fat Chocolate Frosting
	Low-Fat Cream Cheese Frosting
	Low-Fat 7-Minute Frosting
LOW-FAT CHOCOLATE CUPCAKES	Citrus Low-Fat 7-Minute Frosting
	Coffee Low-Fat 7-Minute Frosting
	Low-Fat Chocolate Frosting
	Low-Fat Cream Cheese Frosting
	Low-Fat 7-Minute Frosting
	Peppermint Low-Fat 7-Minute Frosting
LOW-FAT WHITE CUPCAKES	Citrus Low-Fat 7-Minute Frosting
	Coffee Low-Fat 7-Minute Frosting
	Low-Fat Chocolate Frosting
	Low-Fat Cream Cheese Frosting
	Low-Fat 7-Minute Frosting
	Peppermint Low-Fat 7-Minute Frosting
MAPLE WALNUT CUPCAKES	Browned Butter Icing
	Ginger Cream Cheese Frosting
	Maple Cream Cheese Frosting
	Spiked Orange Frosting

MINT CHOCOLATE CHIP CUPCAKES	Champagne Buttercream Icing
	Chocolate Ganache
	Peppermint Cream Cheese Frosting
MOCHA CUPCAKES	Caramel Topping
	Coffee Cream Cheese Frosting
	Mocha Frosting
	Mocha Sauce
	Peppermint Cream Cheese Frosting
	Whipped Cream
OATMEAL RAISIN CUPCAKES	Banana Coconut Frosting
	Cream Cheese Frosting
	Fudge Frosting
	Ginger Cream Cheese Frosting
	Maple Cream Cheese Frosting
ORANGE CUPCAKES	Almond Frosting
	Chocolate Frosting
	Orange Sauce
	Spiked Orange Frosting
	Whipped Cream
PEANUT BUTTER CUPCAKES	Banana Coconut Frosting
	Chocolate Frosting
	Maple Cream Cheese Frosting
	Marshmallow Frosting
	Peanut Butter Frosting
	Strawberry Frosting
PEPPERMINT CUPCAKES	Chocolate Frosting
	Chocolate Ganache
	Peppermint Cream Cheese Frosting

Flavor Combinations and Design Elements ● 239

PEPPERMINT CUPCAKES (*continued*)	Toasted Coconut Cream Cheese Frosting White Chocolate Buttercream Frosting
PEPPERMINT MOCHA CUPCAKES	Cinnamon Whipped Cream Coffee Cream Cheese Frosting Dark Chocolate Icing Mocha Frosting Peppermint Cream Cheese Frosting
PIÑA COLADA CUPCAKES	Coconut Pecan Frosting Lemon Icing Lime Icing Liqueur Icing Rum Syrup Toasted Coconut Cream Cheese Frosting
PINEAPPLE CUPCAKES	Banana Coconut Frosting Ginger Cream CheeseFrosting Liqueur Icing Maple Cream Cheese Frosting Rum Syrup Toasted Coconut Cream Cheese Frosting
PUMPKIN CUPCAKES	Almond Frosting Cinnamon Whipped Cream Maple Cream Cheese Frosting Marzipan Rich Chocolate Frosting
RICH CHOCOLATE CUPCAKES	Almond Frosting Banana Coconut Frosting Chocolate Cream Cheese Frosting Rich Chocolate Frosting

| | White Chocolate Buttercream Frosting |
| | White or Dark Chocolate Ganache |

ROOT BEER CUPCAKES	Maple Cream Cheese Frosting
	Marshmallow Frosting
	Vanilla Frosting

SEA BREEZE CUPCAKES	Lemon Icing
	Lime Icing
	Liqueur Icing
	Rum Syrup

SPICE CUPCAKES	Banana Coconut Frosting
	Coconut Pecan Frosting
	Cream Cheese Frosting
	Maple Cream Cheese Frosting
	Spiked Orange Frosting
	Vanilla Frosting

STRAWBERRY CUPCAKES	Chocolate Macaroon Glaze
	Cream Cheese Frosting
	Fudge Frosting
	Lemon Icing
	Peanut Butter Frosting
	Strawberry Frosting

STRAWBERRY LIME CUPCAKES	Banana Coconut Frosting
	Champagne Buttercream Icing
	Lime Icing
	Rum Syrup
	Strawberry Frosting
	Toasted Coconut Cream Cheese Frosting

| TRES LECHES CUPCAKES | Almond Frosting |
| | Dark Chocolate Sauce |

TRES LECHES CUPCAKES (continued)	Orange, Raspberry or Strawberry Sauce Whipped Cream
VEGAN CHOCOLATE CUPCAKES	Vegan Berry Icing Vegan Chocolate Icing Vegan Coffee Icing Vegan Cream Cheese Icing
VEGAN WHITE CUPCAKES	Vegan Berry Icing Vegan Chocolate Icing Vegan Coffee Icing Vegan Cream Cheese Icing
WHITE CHOCOLATE CUPCAKES	Champagne Buttercream Icing Dark Chocolate Icing Rosewater Icing White Chocolate Buttercream Frosting White or Dark Chocolate Ganache
WHITE CUPCAKES*	Cream Cheese Frosting Fudge Frosting Licorice Frosting Marshmallow Frosting Strawberry Frosting
ZUCCHINI CUPCAKES	Browned Butter Icing Chocolate Frosting Cream Cheese Frosting Ginger Cream Cheese Frosting Lemon Icing Maple Cream Cheese Frosting

*Almost every frosting and icing partners well with this recipe. Try some listed here.

Marbleized and Layered Cupcakes Recipe Combinations

Marbleizing and layering two or three cupcakes recipes is an innovative way to complement flavors. This chart is a handy reference for great cupcakes recipe combinations. Refer to the Cupcakes and Frosting Suggestions Chart for ideas on experimenting with frostings and toppings.

	Taste good with
CHOCOLATE CUPCAKES	Almond Cupcakes
	Banana Cupcakes
	Coffee Cupcakes
	Golden Cupcakes
	Orange Cupcakes
	Peanut Butter Cupcakes
	Peppermint Cupcakes
	White Cupcakes
GOLDEN CUPCAKES	Almond Cupcakes
	Apple Cupcakes
	Champagne Cupcakes
	Chocolate Cupcakes
	Coffee Cupcakes
	Lemon Cupcakes
	Orange Cupcakes
	Spice Cupcakes
	Strawberry Cupcakes
WHITE CUPCAKES	Apple Cupcakes
	Chocolate Cupcakes
	Gingerbread Cupcakes

	Taste good with
WHITE CUPCAKES (*continued*)	Maple Walnut Cupcakes Pumpkin Cupcakes
ALMOND CUPCAKES	Chocolate Cupcakes Coffee Cupcakes Orange Cupcakes
APPLE CUPCAKES	Banana Cupcakes Cranberry Cupcakes Peanut Butter Cupcakes
BANANA CUPCAKES	Maple Walnut Cupcakes Strawberry Cupcakes
BLUEBERRY CUPCAKES	Lemon Cupcakes Orange Cupcakes Strawberry Lime Cupcakes
CHAMPAGNE CUPCAKES	Chocolate Cupcakes Lemon Cupcakes White Chocolate Cupcakes
CHOCOLATE CHOCOLATE CHIP CUPCAKES	Maple Walnut Cupcakes Peppermint Cupcakes White Chocolate Cupcakes
CHOCOLATE RASPBERRY CUPCAKES	Chocolate Cupcakes Golden Cupcakes White Chocolate Cupcakes
COFFEE CUPCAKES	Chocolate Chocolate Chip Cupcakes Eggnog Cupcakes Peppermint Mocha Cupcakes

	Taste good with
CRANBERRY CUPCAKES	Chocolate Cupcakes Gingerbread Cupcakes
EGGNOG CUPCAKES	Chocolate Cupcakes Licorice Cupcakes Spice Cupcakes
GERMAN CHOCOLATE CUPCAKES	Maple Walnut Cupcakes Orange Cupcakes
GINGERBREAD CUPCAKES	Chocolate Cupcakes Eggnog Cupcakes Golden Cupcakes
LEMON CUPCAKES	Low-Fat Carrot Cupcakes Strawberry Cupcakes
LIME CUPCAKES	Lemon Cupcakes Orange Cupcakes Sea Breeze Cupcakes
MAPLE WALNUT CUPCAKES	Chocolate Cupcakes Gingerbread Cupcakes Pumpkin Cupcakes
MOCHA CUPCAKES	Eggnog Cupcakes Golden Cupcakes Kahlúa Cupcakes
ORANGE CUPCAKES	Chocolate Cupcakes Lemon Cupcakes Strawberry Cupcakes

	Taste good with
PEANUT BUTTER CUPCAKES	Banana Cupcakes Chocolate Cupcakes Strawberry Cupcakes
PEPPERMINT CUPCAKES	Mint Chocolate Chip Cupcakes Mocha Cupcakes Rich Chocolate Cupcakes
PUMPKIN CUPCAKES	Chocolate Cupcakes Spice Cupcakes
SPICE CUPCAKES	Apple Cupcakes Maple Walnut Cupcakes Orange Cupcakes
STRAWBERRY CUPCAKES	Apple Cupcakes Blueberry Cupcakes Chocolate Cupcakes
WHITE CHOCOLATE CUPCAKES	Chocolate Cupcakes Strawberry Cupcakes Peppermint Cupcakes
ZUCCHINI CUPCAKES	Low-Fat Carrot Cupcakes Maple Walnut Cupcakes Spice Cupcakes

Mix-In Suggestions

ZESTS	Grapefruit
	Lemon
	Lime
	Orange
CHIPS AND BITS	Butterscotch chips
	Chocolate chips (white, milk, semisweet; mini, regular, large)
	Cinnamon chips
	Mint chips
	Mint chocolate chips
	Peanut butter chips
	Peanut butter chocolate chips
	Toffee bits
CRUSHED COOKIES	Chocolate sandwich cookies
	Gingersnaps
	Graham crackers
	Sugar cones
	Sugar wafers
DRIED FRUITS	Apple rings
	Apricots
	Banana chips
	Currants
	Dates
	Dried bing cherries
	Dried cranberries
	Dried pineapple
	Figs
	Ginger slices
	Guava slices

DRIED FRUITS	Mango slice
(continued)	Papaya slices
	Prunes
	Raisins (golden or brown)
	Shredded or flaked coconut
	Toasted coconut
NUTS	Almonds
	Brazil nuts
	Cashew butter
	Cashews
	Hazelnuts
	Honey-roasted peanuts
	Macadamia nuts
	Party mix
	Peanut butter
	Peanuts
	Pecans
	Pine nuts
	Pumpkin seeds
	Roasted chestnuts
	Sunflower seeds
	Walnuts
FRUITS*	Apples
	Apricots
	Bananas
	Black cherries
	Blueberries
	Cranberries
	Figs
	Fruit cocktail
	Kiwi
	Mandarin oranges

* Fruits can be fresh, canned, or frozen.

Mango
Maraschino cherries
Papaya
Peaches
Pears
Pineapple

CANDIES

Caramels
Carob-covered raisins
Chocolate chunks
Chocolate-covered espresso beans
Chocolate-covered raisins
Chocolate sprinkles
Chopped candy bars
Colored sprinkles
Fruity cereal
Ground butterscotch candies
Ground citrus candies
Ground peppermint candies
Ground root beer candies
Marshmallows
Peanut brittle
Popcorn
Rice cereal
Taffy
Yogurt-covered raisins

JAMS AND JELLIES

Apple butter
Apricot
Apricot pineapple
Black cherry
Black currant
Blackberry
Blueberry
Boysenberry

JAMS AND JELLIES	Cherry
(continued)	Ginger
	Grape
	Kiwi
	Lemon curd
	Mint
	Orange curd
	Orange marmalade
	Peach
	Raspberry
	Raspberry curd
	Strawberry
	Strawberry curd
	White grape
SPICES	Allspice
	Caraway seeds
	Cinnamon
	Fennel seeds
	Ginger
	Mint
	Nutmeg
	Poppy seeds
	Sesame seeds

Cupcake Circle Templates

Different shaped and flavored candies, nuts, zests, fruits, cookies, and dried fruits can be used to create patterns on cupcakes. Here are circle templates to follow for placing your choice of toppings.

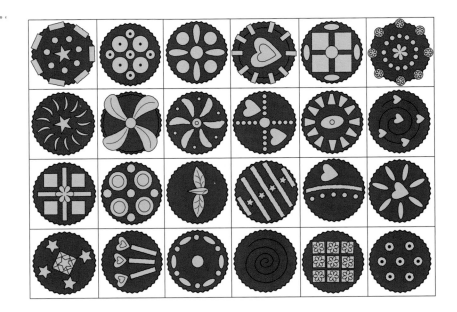

Cupcake Face Templates

Create characters and personalities by placing different shaped and flavored candies and toppings on your cupcakes. Here are face templates to follow for placing your choice of toppings.

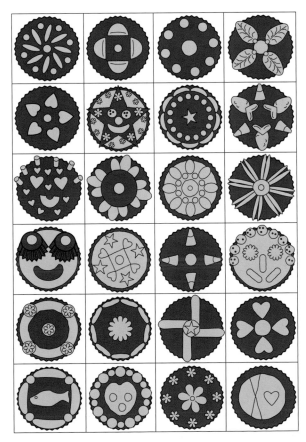

Index

ABOUT THE AUTHOR

Krystina Castella is an industrial designer and professor who designs environments, furniture, clothing, stationery, housewares, toys, and cupcakes. *Crazy About Cupcakes* combines her lifetime love of baking with her design and teaching experience. She lives in Los Angeles, California, with her husband, Brian, and turtle, George.